composing

A STUDENT'S GUIDE

Christopher Binns

Nelson

Thomas Nelson and Sons Ltd
Nelson House Mayfield Road
Walton-on-Thames Surrey
KT12 5PL UK

First published by Thomas Nelson and Sons Ltd 1996.

(ITP) Thomas Nelson is an International Thomson Publishing Company.

(ITP) is used under licence.

ISBN 0-17-436088-6
NPN 9 8 7 6 5 4 3 2

Printed in China

Administration: Eileen Regan
Editorial: Catherine Dakin
Marketing: Jeremy Warner
Production: Tony Warner
Project Coordination: Krystyna Wareing
Staff design: Gabrielle Morton

Acknowledgements

The authors and publishers are grateful to the following for permission to reproduce copyright material. If any acknowledgements have been omitted inadvertently, this will be rectified at the earliest opportunity.

Music:

Bohemian Rhapsody
Words and music by Freddie Mercury.
©1975, Reproduced by permission of B Feldman and Co Ltd trading as Trident Music, London WC2H 0EA.

Honeyman's Tutor
Featured in Wm C Honeyman's 'Strathspey, Reel & Hornpipe Tutor', originally published in 1898 by Honeyman Music Publishing Coy., Newport, Dundee, Scotland, taken here from the facsimile edition published in 1988 by Dragonfly Music, 10 Gibson Street, Newbiggin-by-the-Sea, Northumberland NE64 6PE.

I Know Him So Well
Words and music by Benny Anderson, Björn Ulvaeus and Tim Rice.
Reproduced by permission of Bocu Music Limited.

Last of the Summer Wine
Words by Bill Owen and Roy Clarke, music by Ronnie Hazlehurst.
©1983, Reproduced by permission of EMI Songs Ltd, London WC2H 0EA.

Lovejoy (Theme From)
Music by Denis King.
Reproduced by permission of Eaton Music Limited.

Moonriver
Words by Johnny Mercer, music by Henry Mancini.
©1961 Famous Music Corp, USA.
Warner Chappell Music Ltd, London W1Y 3FA.
Reproduced by permission of International Music Publications Ltd.

Oh Those Britches Full of Stitches!
The Pinch of Snuff
Music arranged by Anthony Sullivan. Featured in *Irish Traditional Music* by Anthony Sullivan.

The Sound of Silence
Words and music by Paul Simon.
©1964 (Renewed) Paul Simon (BMI).
International Copyright Secured All Rights Reserved.
Reprinted by permission.

Telegraph Road
Words and music by Mark Knopfler.
Reproduced by permission of Rondor Music (London) Ltd.

What About Me
Words and music by Chris de Burgh.
Reproduced by permission of Rondor Music (London) Ltd.

Photography:
Hulton Deutsch: pp. 13, 16, 17, 18, 29, 78, 79, 91, 95, 122, 124, 125, 132 (bottom) Range/Bettman/UPI: pp. 78, 131 (top)

Poems and prose:
p. 52: *Winter* Gareth Owen, from *Salford Road and other poems*. Published by Young Lions, 1988. Reproduced by permission of the author c/o Rogers, Coleridge & White Ltd.
p. 74: *Lullaby* Adrian Henri, from *Penguin Modern Poets 10: The Mersey Sound*. Published by Kestrel Books. Reproduced by permission of the author c/o Rogers, Coleridge & White Ltd., 20 Powis Mews, London W11 1JN.
Street Boy Gareth Owen, from *Salford Road and other poems*. Published by Young Lions, 1988. Reproduced by permission of the author c/o Rogers, Coleridge & White Ltd.
p. 76: *Cider with Rosie* Laurie Lee. Published by Chatto & Windus.
p. 77: *Under Milk Wood* Dylan Thomas. Published by JM Dent & Sons Ltd.

The author gratefully acknowledges the contributions made by the following people: Margaret Binns, John Harris, J Godfrey Turner, Philip Taylor, Chris Cook, Andrew Coxon, Brian Quinn, Paul Wilson, Catherine E Binns, H Claire Binns.

Contents

Skills, approaches and assignments

Rudiments and reference

1

What makes a good melody?

Being able to compose a good melody for an instrument or a voice, or a group of instruments or voices, is part of the composer's craft. A great deal can be learnt by looking at, and listening to, the melodies of other composers. A study of some well-known tunes will show that there are several important elements to be considered in creating a successful melody. These elements determine the character of the music and include: **range, key (mode or scale), length, shape, rhythm, time signature,** and **performance details** such as **tempo, dynamics, expression marks** and **mood.**

This chapter gives information about these **musical elements.** Chapter 2 helps you apply this knowledge in your own compositions, while Chapter 3 illustrates the importance of repetition. Chapter 4 provides information about the use of **modulation** and **embellishments.**

As a starting point, look at the selection of melodies on pages 1–6. Some are printed in full, while others are only excerpts. If you have not heard them before, play or sing the melodies for yourself or ask your teacher to help. The melodies illustrate some of the ways in which composers have used the various elements which all contribute to an effective melody.

A melody or tune is a series of notes, organised into a pattern of rhythms and pitch which has a musical shape. A melody may occur on its own, or may be combined with one or more melodies, or it may be supported by harmonies.

Figure 1.1

A   *God Save the Queen*   Origin uncertain

B   *All Through the Night*   Welsh Traditional

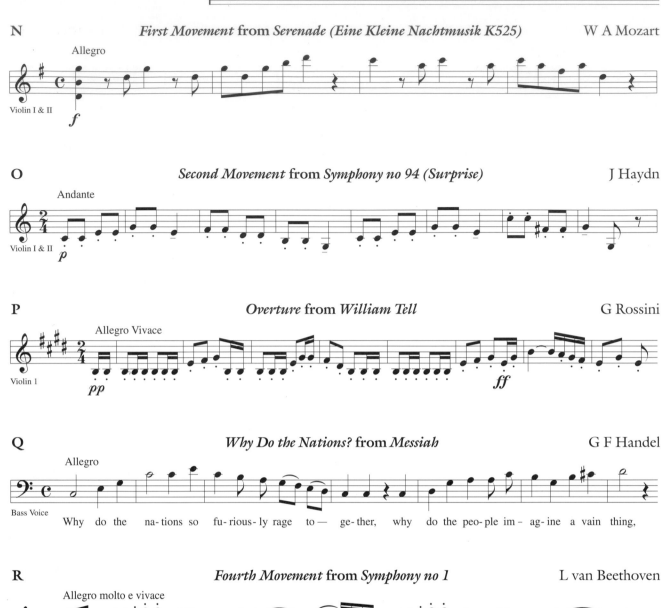

N   *First Movement* **from** *Serenade (Eine Kleine Nachtmusik K525)*   W A Mozart

O   *Second Movement* **from** *Symphony no 94 (Surprise)*   J Haydn

P   *Overture* **from** *William Tell*   G Rossini

Q   *Why Do the Nations?* **from** *Messiah*   G F Handel

Why do the na- tions so fu- rious- ly rage to — ge- ther, why do the peo- ple im – ag- ine a vain thing,

R   *Fourth Movement* **from** *Symphony no 1*   L van Beethoven

S   *Second Movement* **from** *String Quartet Opus 76 no 3 (Emperor)*   J Haydn

T   *Miniature Overture* from *The Nutcracker Suite*   P I Tchaikovsky

U   *Morning* from *Peer Gynt Suite*   E Grieg

V   *Over the Rainbow*   music by Howard Arlen
words by E Y Harburg

Some - where o - ver the rain - bow way up high, There's a land that I heard of once in a lul - la - by.

W   *Fourth Movement* from *Symphony no 1*   J Brahms

X   *Prélude* from *L'Arlésienne, Suite No 1*   G Bizet

Y   *First Movement* from *Symphony no. 40, K550*   W A Mozart

Z

I Know Him So Well **from** *Chess*

music and lyrics by
Benny Andersson, Björn
Ulvaeus and Tim Rice

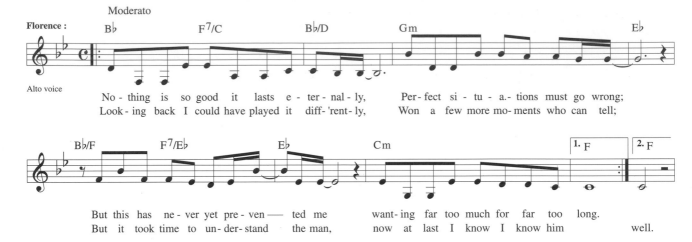

Florence :

Alto voice

No - thing is so good it lasts e - ter - nal - ly,   Per - fect si - tu - a - tions must go wrong;
Look - ing back I could have played it diff- 'rent- ly,   Won a few more mo- ments who can tell;

But this has ne - ver yet pre - ven —— ted me   want- ing far too much for far too long.
But it took time to un- der- stand   the man,   now at last I know I know him   well.

Range

When we talk about the **range** of a melody we are referring to the selection of notes used from the lowest in pitch to the highest. For example, the range of tune A in Figure 1.1, *God Save the Queen* is from F# (first space in the treble clef) to E (top space).

When composing a melody it is important to know the range of notes that are available, or suitable, for the instrument or voice that will perform the music. You must avoid using notes that are outside this range. Some instruments have a very wide range (or **compass**) and produce different qualities of sound within their register. For example, the clarinet in the lower register has a deep and resonant tone, while the middle register is rich and powerful, and the upper register more strident or piercing.

Tune B, *All Through the Night* (page 1), has a slightly wider range than tune A, *God Save the Queen* from D (below the stave) to E (top space). *All Through the Night* is a vocal melody, which fits the soprano or treble voice

Figure 1.2 : A melody written for violin. Jack's the Lad is a hornpipe, a lively dance with two beats in the bar. The range covers two octaves from B♭ below the stave (bar 1) to B♭ above the stave (bar 5). This range is ideal for the violin and well within the compass of the instrument.

The College Hornpipe **or** *Jack's the Lad*

Traditional

Violin

very comfortably. The range is also suitable for a number of instruments including the recorder, clarinet or trumpet. Tune C, from *Vltava*, has a range of just over one octave, from B (middle line) to C (two ledger lines). It is written here for violins and oboe and extends higher than would normally be written for a soprano, although it is quite playable by both instruments.

As well as being aware of the range of the voice or instrument that you are composing for, you should also ensure that written music has a suitable clef (see page 167). Tune G, *The Elephant*, was written for the double bass and has a **bass clef,** while tune J, *Gavotte*, for violins and oboes, has a **treble clef.** Tune X, for violas, features the **alto clef,** in this extract from the *Prélude from L'Arlésienne, Suite No 1*.

ASSIGNMENTS

1 Comment on the range of some of the melodies on pages 1–6.

2 For each melody that you have chosen, name an instrument or voice other than the one indicated, which could perform the music. For instance, Example U, *Morning*, is written for flute, but could also be played by an oboe, clarinet or violin.

3 Select a number of pieces of music of your own choice written for voice or different instruments:

    a Find one instrumental melody written on a single stave (rather than two staves, such as piano music) and comment on the range of notes.

    b Find a vocal melody and comment on the range of notes.

    c Find some music written for a keyboard instrument such as a piano or organ, and comment on the range of notes used.

    d Find a longer piece of music, such as a whole movement, written for any instrument or voice and comment on the range of notes used throughout the music.

    e Compare the range of one of the melodies you have already chosen, with the compass of the instrument for which the music is written. Does the music fit comfortably within the instrument's compass, or does it reach the extremes of its range?

    (You may wish to consult the *Rudiments and Reference* section which provides information about the compass of many instruments and voices.)

Key, mode, other scales and atonal melodies

The pitch of each melody note, and the order in which each note in the melody is placed are of great importance. The choice of notes will be governed by the key or scale upon which the melody is based. Melodies frequently have a **tonality**, being composed in a **major** or **minor** key, although there are other alternatives. For example, a melody may be either based upon one of the **modes** or **another type of scale**. Alternatively, the melody may be **atonal**.

Key: A melody may be written in a major or minor key. The notes used (although others may be added) will be those found in the appropriate diatonic major or minor scale.

Mode: Modes were an early form of scales. Each mode contains 8 notes and has two forms, the *authentic* and the *plagal*. For example, the authentic Dorian mode consists of the notes **D E F G A B C D.**

Other scales: A melody may be based upon a scale that is neither diatonic nor modal. There are many other such scales, and they occur frequently in Western music, and in music of other cultures around the world. Two examples are the *pentatonic* or *five-note* scale, and the *whole-tone* scale.

Atonal melodies: Atonal music does not have a tonality, or feeling of key. Such music includes *twelve-note music* with the melody based upon a *tone row*.

Information about keys and scales can be found in the *Rudiments and Reference* section. Modal music, pentatonic music, and music built on the whole-tone scale are explained, together with assignments, in later chapters. Here, we focus upon melodies which are written in a major or minor key.

More about keys

A melody can be composed in any key although there are a few basic points to consider.

- Tunes in a **major** key will have a different character from tunes in a **minor** key. Major keys are often described as 'bright', 'positive', and 'happy', while minor keys are referred to as 'dark', 'ominous' and 'sad'. For example, in Figure 1.3, the first eight bars of *John Peel*, a lively, jolly tune, are written in the key of D major.

Figure 1.3

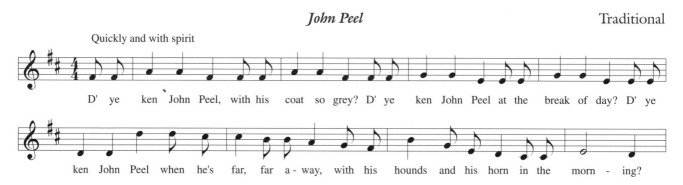

John Peel   Traditional

Quickly and with spirit

D' ye   ken   John Peel,   with his   coat   so grey? D' ye   ken   John Peel   at the   break of day? D' ye

ken   John Peel   when   he's   far,   far a-way,   with his   hounds   and his   horn   in the   morn - ing?

Tune G, *The Elephant* (page 2), in the key of E♭ major, presents a cheerful and humorous musical portrait of the elephant and tune P, a theme from *The William Tell Overture* in the key of E major, is energetic and rousing. In contrast, *The Miller of Dee* is written in G minor, and the melody has a somewhat melancholic character.

Figure 1.4

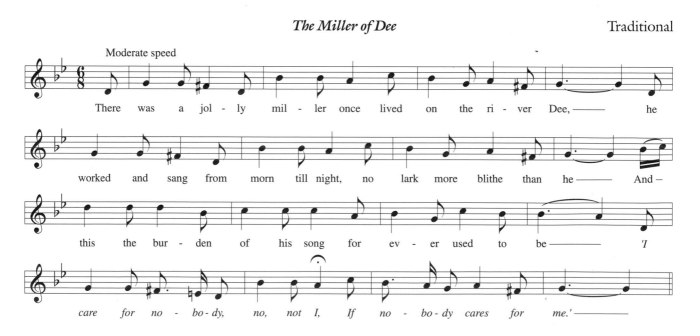

The Miller of Dee   Traditional

Moderate speed

There   was   a   jol - ly   mil - er   once   lived   on   the   ri - ver   Dee, ——— he

worked   and   sang   from   morn   till   night,   no   lark   more   blithe   than   he ——— And —

this   the   bur - den   of   his   song   for   ev - er   used   to   be ———   'I

care   for   no - bo - dy,   no,   not   I,   If   no - bo - dy   cares   for   me.' ———

Some of the tunes on pages 1–6 also provide examples of melodies written in a minor key. Tune E, *O Sacred Head, Surrounded*, in the key of D minor, is a fine example of a simple melody which conveys great sadness, while tune D, the theme from *Danse Macabre*, which occasionally impishly moves away from the key of G minor, has a haunting and dark character. Tune Y is taken from the first movement of Mozart's *Symphony No 40*. This melody for violins is in the key of G minor, and has an anxious and sombre quality. Tune C, from *Vltava* is also written in a minor key. Here, the melody appears in the key of E minor, representing the restless quality of the River Vltava. Listen to the whole of this orchestral piece of music if you can, to see how the composer, Bedřich Smetana, transformed the character of this theme by finally presenting it in the major key. The change in key suggests the broad and majestic progress of the river as it reaches the city of Prague after its lengthy journey.

- Many melodies quickly establish the tonic key either by starting on the tonic note (the key note), or by putting the tonic as the first beat of the first complete bar. For example, the folk song *Early One Morning* begins on the tonic note F. The melody of *The Ash Grove* in the key of G major, has the tonic note G as the first beat of the first complete bar, preceded by the dominant note D. (The technical names for the degrees of a major and minor scale such as **tonic** and **dominant** are shown on page 176.)

Early One Morning   English Folk Song   *Figure 1.5*

The Ash Grove   Welsh Traditional   *Figure 1.6*
words by Thomas Oliphant

Tune A of Figure 1.1, *God Save the Queen* (page 1), is written in the key of G major which begins on the note G, and tune E, *O Sacred Head, Surrounded,* is in the key of D minor, which has the note D as the first beat of the first complete bar.

Many melodies, like *Auld Lang Syne* in Figure 1.7, finish on the tonic note. *God Save the Queen* of Figure 1.1 and tune B, *All Through the Night*, are both written in the key of G major, each melody beginning and ending with the tonic note G.

Figure 1.7   *Auld Lang Syne*   Scottish Traditional tune

- A melody can *modulate*, or move, to another key or a number of other keys. Sometimes the music only passes into the new key very briefly, and returns immediately to the original key. In Figure 1.8, for example, the melody of *Winchester Old (While Shepherds Watched Their Flocks By Night)* moves very briefly from the key of F major to the key of C major, but then immediately returns to F major. The modulation in this example is signalled by the appearance of an **accidental**, the **natural** sign, in bar 3.

An accidental is a *sharp, flat, double sharp, double flat* or *natural* sign which occurs in the music but is not in the key signature.

Figure 1.8   *Winchester Old*   (Later version of melody from Thomas Este's Psalter, 1592)

In moderate time

Once the new key is established, the melody could remain there for longer. Figure 1.9, from a *piano sonatina* by Clementi, is in the key of G major. By bar 8, it has modulated to the key of D major, where it remains for a further 14 bars. In nearly every case, music that modulates to a new key or a number of new keys, returns to, and ends in, the original key. Tunes I, L, O, Q, and R of Figure 1.1 provide further examples of melodies which feature a modulation. Additional information about modulation can be found in Chapter 4.

- The key should be suitable for the instrument and performer. Some keys may present difficulties for particular instruments. Keys with a large number of sharps should be avoided when writing for brass instruments, for example. Performers, too, should be considered when choosing a key for the melody. A singer, for example, will have a particular vocal range and it would be unwise to choose a key that resulted in the vocalist having to sing notes much higher or lower than

Sonatina in G Op. 36 no. 2   M Clementi   *Figure 1.9*

he or she would normally attempt. Tune Q, *Why Do the Nations?* is ideally suited to the bass voice, but may be at an inappropriate pitch for a contralto!

• When deciding upon a key or keys for your composition, do not forget to consider the ability of the performers who will play your music. For example, beginner instrumentalists (on some instruments) may not be able to produce the full range of notes from their instruments. Music written in some keys may therefore be difficult for them to play. Beginners may also find keys that have lots of sharps or flats difficult to cope with.

ASSIGNMENTS

1 Excluding tunes I, L, O and Q, name the keys of all the melodies on pages 1–6.

2 Name the keys of tune I, *The Trout*, tune L, *Bourrée*, tune O, *Second Movement Theme from the Surprise Symphony*, and tune Q, *Why Do the Nations?* Name the key to which each melody modulates.

3 Find a piece of music of your own choice. State the key of the music and list any modulations which occur.

4 Using any vocal or instrumental music of your own choice, find three pieces with a melody which begins on the tonic note, or has the tonic note as the first beat of the bar.

5 Using any vocal or instrumental music of your own choice, find three pieces with a melody which ends on the tonic note.

Length

A melody can be of any length and occupy any number of bars. It can also be extended and developed as necessary. While there are no strict rules about the length of a melody, many have an even number of bars, the most frequent being eight, 12, 16, 24 and 32 bars.

Often, the melody can be further sub-divided into regular phrases, which are natural divisions of the melodic line. Phrases are frequently two, four or eight bars in length, although of course they may be of any length. Many melodies also have repeats or include repeated sections.

A *strathspey* is a slow Scottish dance in $\frac{4}{4}$ time with many dotted rhythms.

Figure 1.10 shows a strathspey, *The Duchess of Gordon*. The melody is 16 bars in length, consisting of a repeated four-bar section, followed by an eight-bar section. The entire melody would then be repeated as many times as necessary, possibly with some variations. Each four-bar division, or phrase, of this strathspey could be further divided into two balanced two-bar phrases. One of the characteristics of this melody is the use of repeated phrases, or parts of phrases. Many individual bars are repeated, being identical, or very similar, in rhythm and pitch. The importance of repeated rhythms and rhythm patterns is discussed later in this chapter.

Figure 1.10   *The Duchess of Gordon*   Strathspey
(from Wm C Honeyman's Tutor)

In the *Hornpipe* from G F Handel's *Water Music* (Figure 1.11), the repeats extend the piece considerably. The first eight bars of the melody repeat (making 16 bars), as do the next eight bars (making another 16 bars). These 32 bars are then repeated fully, usually played by a different small group of instruments to provide a contrast. Finally, the entire 32 bars are repeated again, making a total of 96 bars in all.

Tune B of Figure 1.1, *All Through the Night,* provides another example. It has a four-bar repeated melody, followed by an eight-bar section which itself includes a repeat of the opening melody. In total, 16 bars are neatly divided into four-bar phrases.

Figure 1.11   *Hornpipe* from *The Water Music*   G F Handel

Violin 1 / Oboe 1

Not all melodies are constructed in such a regular way as the above examples. Many melodies have phrases of varying lengths which are not eight, 12, 24 or 32 bars in length. While the composer must give careful thought to the length of a melody, the phrases within it, and the use of repeats, the main consideration when composing a melody is that it must sound effective.

ASSIGNMENTS

Using music of your own choice, find examples of the following:

  a an eight-bar vocal melody, such as a folk song or hymn.

  b a 16-bar vocal melody comprising two different eight-bar sections.

  c a 16-bar instrumental piece. The music may be for a solo instrument without accompaniment, or for an instrument in an ensemble.

  d an instrumental piece comprising two sections of different lengths, such as eight bars plus 16 bars, which may, or may not be repeated.

  e a composition longer than 16 bars which includes repeated sections.

  f a vocal or instrumental composition which is not eight, 12, 16, 24 or 32 bars in length.

G F Handel (1685–1759)

Shape

The shape of a melody includes a consideration of the intervals between each adjacent note of the melody. (Intervals are explained on page 180.) Some melodies move smoothly, step by step, up one note or down one note (by the interval of a 2nd) as the tune progresses. Look at Figure 1.12, *Good King Wenceslas*. Although the melodic movement is not entirely step-wise, most notes in this melody do move only up or down by step, or repeat the previous note.

Now study tunes A, *God Save the Queen*, B, *All Through the Night*, C, *Vltava*, and D, *Danse Macabre* in Figure 1.1, and note that all these melodies feature mostly step-wise movement. Some melodies feature a

The shape of a melody generally refers to the pattern, or rise and fall, of the notes in the melodic line.

Figure 1.12   *Good King Wenceslas*   Traditional

succession of step-wise notes, such as scale passages, or scale-like passages. Tune R, from the *Fourth Movement* of *Beethoven's First Symphony*, illustrates this point.

There are many melodies which do not move by step. A variety of intervals occurs between adjacent melody notes, and leaps of up to an octave are commonly found. Tunes J, *Gavotte* and V, *Over the Rainbow* of Figure 1.1, show this feature.

The most frequent intervals between adjacent melody notes are leaps of a second, third or a fourth. The opening bars of a traditional Irish melody, *The Pinch of Snuff* (Figure 1.13), move almost entirely by the intervals of a second, third and fourth.

Figure 1.13   *The Pinch of Snuff*   Irish Traditional
                                                                                                          (arr. Anthony Sullivan)

As we have already seen when considering the key of a melody, the first two notes of some tunes are the dominant and tonic notes. The interval between these two notes is called a **perfect 4th.** Tunes C, D, E, F, G, H, I and W of Figure 1.1 all begin in this way.

Most melodies will contain a mixture of interval leaps and step-wise movement depending upon the character of the music. Too much step-wise movement can become repetitive and tedious, while frequent leaps of large intervals can be difficult to perform and unsatisfying to the ear. The first 16 bars of *Moon River* contain a variety of intervals between the melody notes.

Figure 1.14 *Moon River* music by Henri Mancini
words by Johnny Mercer

ASSIGNMENTS

1 Using four of the tunes in Figure 1.1 (excluding tune Z), comment on the shape of the melodies which you have chosen.

2 Describe the intervals found between the melody notes of *Moon River*. Comment on the variety of intervals which are used.

3 Tune Z of Figure 1.1, *I Know Him So Well*, contains some repeated notes, but also has quite a variety of intervals between adjacent melody notes. How many different intervals can you find between adjacent notes of this melody?

4 Using music of your own choice, find examples of the following:
   a a vocal melody which contains mainly step-wise movement.
   b an instrumental melody which contains mainly step-wise movement.
   c a vocal melody which moves mostly by intervals greater than a 2nd.
   d an instrumental melody which moves mostly by intervals greater than a 2nd.

Rhythm

The rhythm of the melody is a very important ingredient, which adds much to its character. Notes of any time value can be used, although it is not always necessary to have a great variety of time values and rhythms. Many tunes work well because the composer has used a few carefully selected rhythmic ideas and has repeated or developed these, rather than adding lots of new rhythms as the tune progresses. Figure 1.10, *The Duchess of Gordon*, illustrates this point, as does the minuet by J S Bach (Figure 1.15). Although Figure 1.15 was originally composed for a keyboard instrument, the melody is often arranged for other instruments such as recorder, flute or violin. The first 16 bars of the minuet are shown. While the composer has used mainly crotchets and quavers in this piece of music, the repeated rhythmic patterns of these notes give the music a sense of unity and balance.

Figure 1.15   *Minuet* from *the Anna Magdalena Notebook*   J S Bach

Another example is taken from W A Mozart's opera, *Die Zauberflöte* (*The Magic Flute*). This beautiful melody for bass voice is rhythmically uncomplicated, yet it is the simplicity of the rhythm, together with the melodic shape and the slow tempo, which makes this **aria** (song) so effective (Figure 1.16).

Refer to some of the melodies featured at the beginning of this chapter. For example, tune D of Figure 1.1 from *Danse Macabre* simply uses crotchets and minims to produce a flowing melody in waltz time, while tune L, *Bourrée*, is written in crotchets and quavers, except for the final dotted minim.

A significant feature of many melodies is that they will often finish on a long note, unless the composer wants a particular 'clipped' or **staccato** effect. Two complete melodies, *God Save the Queen* and *All Through the Night* of Figure 1.1, both finish on long notes.

If the composition begins with an incomplete bar, with one or more notes occurring before the first beat of the first complete bar, it is customary to make up the correct number of beats in the final bar, so that the first and last bars added together make one complete whole bar. Tune L of Figure 1.1, from *The Water Music*, does this, and the weak beat opening is called an **anacrusis**.

W A Mozart (1756–1791)

Figure 1.16   *Aria: O Isis und Osiris, schenket der Weisheit Geist* from *The Magic Flute*   W A Mozart

Rests can also play an important part in a melody. Their inclusion is sometimes for practical reasons, for example allowing the singer or performer on a wind instrument an opportunity to breathe. Composers often use rests to enhance a melody or to produce a desired effect. In Figure 1.1, tunes K, *Theme from the Enigma Variations*, N, from *Eine Kleine Nachtmusik*, T, from *The Nutcracker Suite*, and X, *Prélude from L'Arlésienne Suite No.1*, each features rests. The three melodies in Figure 1.17 also illustrate the effective use of rests.

Figure 1.17a

Second subject from
The Hebrides Overture   F Mendelssohn-Bartholdy

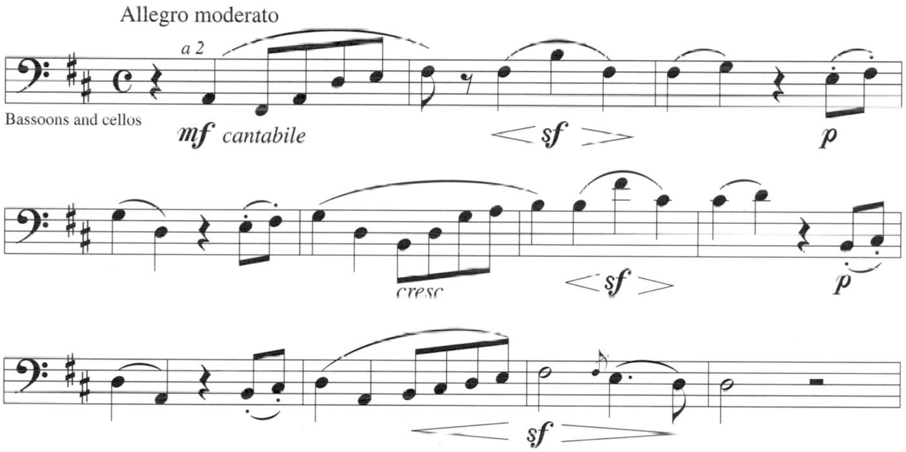

Figure 1.17b

First movement from
Symphony no 92 (Oxford)   J Haydn

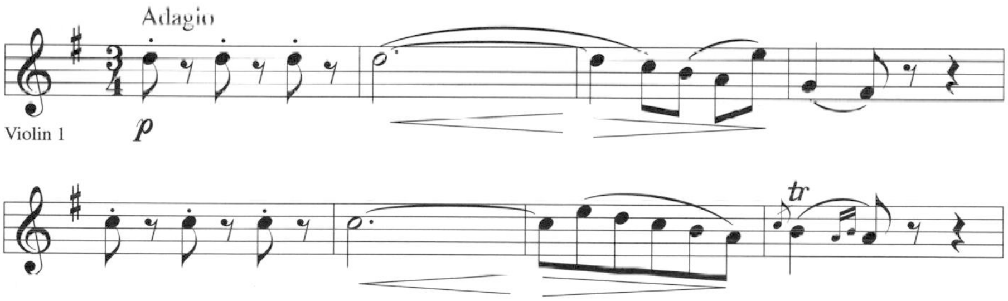

L van Beethoven (1770–1827)

Figure 1.17c

First movement from
Symphony no 4   L van Beethoven

Repeated rhythm patterns can be found in many melodies. As we have already seen in the Bach *Minuet* (Figure 1.15) and the Mozart *Aria* (Figure 1.16), a rhythmic phrase can be repeated or slightly changed, or it can suggest a rhythmic answer. In this way it provides the rhythmic structure for most or all of the melody. Repeated rhythm patterns are used in Figure 1.18, *The Mallow Fling*. Tune M from Dvořák's *Symphony No. 9*, tune P from *The William Tell Overture*, tune T from *The Nutcracker Suite* and tune Y from Mozart's *Symphony No. 40*, all contain repeated rhythm patterns.

Figure 1.18

The Mallow Fling   Traditional

ASSIGNMENTS

1 Comment on the rhythm of the following extracts:
  a Tune B, *All Through the Night*.
  b Tune O, from Haydn's *Surprise Symphony*.
  c Tune W from Brahms' *First Symphony*.

2 Using music of your own choice, find examples of:
  a a vocal melody which features repeated rhythmic patterns.
  b an instrumental melody which features repeated rhythmic patterns.
  c a vocal melody which includes rests.
  d an instrumental melody which includes rests.
  e a vocal melody which begins with an anacrusis.
  f an instrumental melody which begins with an anacrusis.

J Haydn (1732–1809)

Time signature

The time signature appears at the beginning of the written music. In many melodies, the number of beats in a bar and the time value of the beat indicated by the time signature, will not change throughout the entire composition. In the following traditional melody (Figure 1.19), which may be repeated as many times as appropriate, the time signature is unchanged throughout.

Figure 1.19   *Oh Those Britches Full of Stitches!*   Irish Traditional
(arr. Anthony Sullivan)

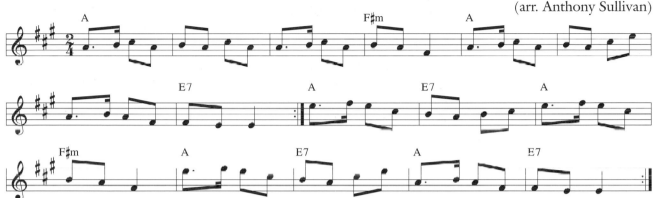

The time signature may change during a composition. If it does so, the new time signature must be added to indicate this. The time signature could change frequently in a composition, and sometimes even in consecutive bars, as shown in Figure 1.20.

Theme from Second movement, *Symphony no. 9*   Dmitri Shostakovich

Clarinet 1 in A

When composing your own melody, you may wish to establish the time signature or the number of beats in a bar, before you begin, particularly if you decide that the time signature will not change during the piece. For example, you could choose to compose a waltz in $\frac{3}{4}$ time, or a march in $\frac{4}{4}$ time. Knowing the time signature before you begin can sometimes help you to produce your music more efficiently.

Some composers work out the music first, listening, experimenting with the sounds and developing musical ideas before any consideration is given to a time signature. In such cases, the final choice about an appropriate time signature (or time signatures) in the written score may only be decided *when the composition is complete*. More information about time signatures can be found on pages 171–173.

Figure 1.20: The instruction ♩ = ♩ **in this example, means that the crotchet beats have the same time value and duration in both $\frac{3}{4}$ and $\frac{4}{4}$ (C = common time = $\frac{4}{4}$).**

ASSIGNMENTS

1 Find six pieces of music of your own choice, each with a different time signature. The time signatures of your chosen music should not change during the piece.

2 Find two examples of music that have more than one time signature. The change(s) of time signature should occur within a single movement or section of a composition.

Performance details

Tempo

When composing a melody, it is important to decide upon an appropriate speed or tempo. The tempo may either remain constant throughout the music, or it may change. If you intend to write out your melody, the tempo and any subsequent change of the tempo must be clearly stated in the written score of your music. Although Italian words such as **allegro**, **adagio**, or **vivace** are often used to indicate the required tempo, you may see the tempo and performance instructions written in other languages, especially German, French or English. A list of many of the words used to indicate tempo can be found on pages 184–186. The tempo mark is usually written above the music as in Figure 1.21. You may also add a metronome mark such as ♩. = 108 to show more precisely the speed of the beat.

Figure 1.21

Theme from Third movement,
Symphony No. 6   L van Beethoven

Any tempo can be chosen for your melodies and compositions, although some consideration should be given to the abilities of the performer(s), particularly if a fast or lively tempo is required. Inexperienced instrumentalists and singers may also encounter difficulties with breath control and phrasing if the tempo is quite slow.

> The metronome mark indicates the exact number of beats in one minute; in Figure 1.21 the metronome mark means that there are 108 dotted-minim beats per minute.

While you may find music that does not have a tempo marking (such as some folk music and some music composed up to, and including, the time of Bach and Handel), it is always a good idea to give a clear indication of the tempo of your own composition.

ASSIGNMENTS

1 Explain the tempo marks in the following tunes in Figure 1.1: tune G, *The Elephant* by Saint-Saëns, tune M from Dvořák's *Symphony No. 9*, tune R from Beethoven's *Symphony No.1*, and tune Y from Mozart's *Symphony No.40*.

2 For Assignments **a, b, c** and **d**, find examples of tempo marks in music of your own choice. For each example, give the title of the music, the name of the composer, and the instrument(s) or voice(s) for which the music is written.

For Assignments **a, b** and **c**, explain the tempo marks written in Italian, German and French.

a Find four examples of music, each with a different tempo written in Italian.

b Find four examples of music, each with a different tempo written in German.

c Find four examples of music, each with a different tempo written in French.

d Find four examples of music each with a different tempo written in English.

3 Find four examples of music which do not have a tempo mark or indication of speed.

    a Give the title of each piece of music, the name of the composer (if known), and the instruments or voices for which the music was written.

    b Suggest reasons why each of these pieces does not have a tempo indication written on the score.

    c Suggest a suitable tempo for each piece.

Dynamics and expression marks

Dynamics and expression marks add to the character and mood of the melody. Some melodies may feature only a few dynamics or expression marks, while others require many. The addition of these performance instructions gives light and shade to a composition, and in any score of your music care should be taken to write them accurately. Tune K of Figure 1.1, the extract from Elgar's *Enigma Variations*, contains detailed performance instructions, as does Figure 1.22. A list of words and signs which are used to indicate dynamics, expression and style can be seen in the *Rudiments and Reference* section (pages 184–186).

Dynamics refers to the intensity of sound.

Danse Russe: Trepak from *The Nutcracker Suite*　P Tchaikovsky

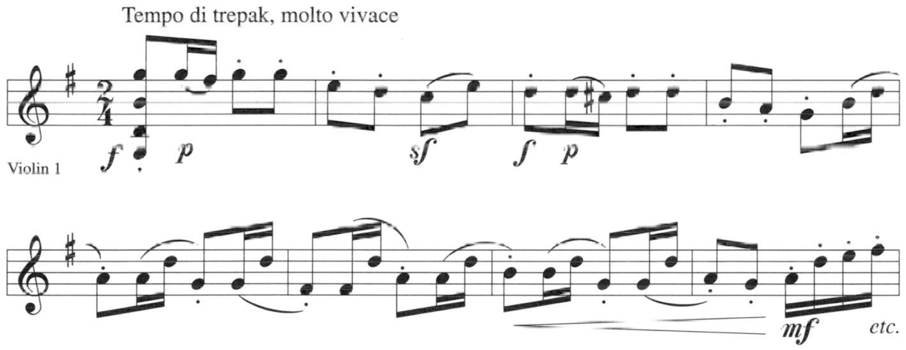

Figure 1.22

ASSIGNMENTS

1 Find four melodies which contain dynamic marks, or expression marks, and for each give the title of the music, the instrument or voice for which it is written, and the composer's name.

2 Choose one of these four melodies.

    a Explain the meaning of all the performance details which are written on the music.

    b Suggest alternative dynamic marks or expression marks which you think would work well with the music. If possible, play or sing the melody adding the original dynamic and expression marks, and then adding your own.

3 Find four pieces of music which do not have any dynamic marks or marks of expression.

a Give the name of each piece, the name of the composer (if known) and the instrument(s) or voice(s) for which the music is written.

b Suggest reasons why each of these pieces does not contain dynamic marks or marks of expression.

Suggest some appropriate dynamic marks and expression marks for each piece.

Mood

The mood or character of the melody or composition will be achieved by the appropriate use of some, or all, of the different elements that we have discussed in this chapter. The range of notes, the shape of the melody, the rhythms which you use and your choice of key (or mode or scale), time signature(s), tempo (or tempi), dynamics and expression marks, will all contribute to the mood and character of your music.

The way in which your melody is developed or extended with *sequence* or *repetition* or enhanced with *modulation* or *embellishments*, may also add to its mood. These aspects are dealt with in the following chapters.

The mood or character may, of course, be apparent in the title of the music, and may also be indicated by a written performance instruction such as **agitato** (agitated), **tranquillo** (calm) and **lacrimoso** (sad).

ASSIGNMENTS

1 Make a list of ten melodies or compositions with descriptive titles which give an indication of the mood or character of the music. Name the composer of each and state the instrument(s) or voice(s) for which each piece was written.

2 Listen to one of the pieces that you have named above and suggest six ways in which the composer has achieved the mood of the music.

SUMMARY ASSIGNMENTS

1 Write about a piece of music of your own choice, including the following points:

a State the title of the music, the name of the composer and the instruments or voices for which the music is intended.

b Comment upon the following aspects of the melody:
range; key (or mode or scale upon which the melody is based); length; shape; rhythm; time signature(s); tempo (or tempi); dynamic marks and marks of expression; mood; any other points of interest

c Describe how the above features contribute to the character of the piece.

2 Listen to, or perform, the music you have chosen.

2

Now compose a melody

To compose your own melodies and achieve the mood or character that you require, you will have to consider the elements discussed in the previous chapter. Decide upon the most appropriate range of notes and rhythms, length of melody, key or mode, time signature, tempo, dynamics and expression marks. Consider who is going to perform your music, and take into account their performing skills.

The process of composition

It is important to hear or imagine your music and know exactly how it will sound before writing it down. With practice, you should be able to hear and organise these sounds in your head (without an instrument) but this is not a requirement for beginners! Unless you can imagine the sounds, the process of composing involves trying out your ideas on an instrument (or singing them). The process of composing will then involve trying out different melody notes, and experimenting with alternative rhythms, dynamics and phrasing until eventually the melody is finished.

You do not necessarily have to work with single melody notes as you try out different ideas. You may find that working with chords and harmonies helps you to produce your melody, even though ultimately they may not be used to accompany the completed music.

Sometimes, as you work on your melody, you may make only slight changes to your original ideas, but occasionally you will discover new and exciting possibilities that you will want to explore. You may also discover musical ideas that you would want to write down or record to save for future compositions.

Results may come quickly, or take some time. If you feel that you are not making progress, leave it for a while and then go back to it. You must be prepared to work on your composition and change things which are not satisfactory. Always be thorough and critical in your work and don't hurry the process of composition just to finish quickly.

Although there are many different ways to approach composition, two possible methods of composing a melody are given here. Either method is appropriate, and each can be adapted to suit your own preferred way of working. Methods 1 and 2 are simple guidelines, not rules.

Method 1: Starting without a plan

One approach to composing is to extemporise, or experiment, on an instrument (or with your voice), starting with no definite plan about the type of melody or composition that you want. As ideas come to mind, try them out and then either discard them, put them aside for future use, or modify or develop them until eventually you are satisfied with the outcome.

During this process of experimentation, decide about the various elements or components of the melody, such as the mood, the tonality, the tempo and the dynamics. The choice of instrument or performer most suitable for the composition may be left until the melody is complete. This is a very flexible, open-ended method of working, placing no restrictions nor constraints upon the composer.

Method 2: Starting with a plan

A second approach to composing is more structured and pre-planned than method 1. It requires that certain decisions are taken before the practical working-out of ideas on the instrument (or voice) begins. This procedure directs the composer's efforts in a more controlled and pre-determined manner.

The actual working-out process is the same in both approaches. However, in the second method, some preparation is required before the practical experimentation takes place. Also, some of the outcomes must be decided at the beginning of the process, rather than during or after it. The following plan outlines this second method:

Preparation

1 **Choose an instrument or type of voice.**

   a What is the range of the instrument or voice? (See *Rudiments and Reference* section if you wish to check.)

   b Will it be an unaccompanied melody or will you add an accompaniment? For the moment, we will compose an unaccompanied melody. If you wish to add an accompaniment, consider:

   - Which instrument will play the accompaniment? In some cases, it may be the same instrument. For example, a melody for electronic keyboard or piano could be accompanied by chords or harmonies on the same instrument. Alternatively, it may be a different instrument. For example, a solo for flute might be accompanied by piano or guitar.
   - Which chords or harmonies would you use?
   - How will the accompaniment and melody work together?

c Who will perform the composition? Does this affect the range of notes which can be used, the key, the speed, the difficulty of the piece or the length of the composition?

2 Decide upon the following:

a Title

b Mood or character of the music

c Key, mode or scale. Your melody could be:
   * in a major or minor key
   * modal
   * based on the pentatonic or five-note scale
   * based on the whole-tone scale

d Style

e Tempo

f Time signature

g Rhythm

You may choose a rhythm or rhythm patterns before you begin, or prefer to wait until you try out your ideas on your instrument or with your voice. In some cases, the style or type of music which you have chosen may suggest a rhythm. Dances, for example, such as the gavotte, tango or strathspey each have their own characteristic rhythm patterns.

h Length

i Form

Forms refers to the plan of the music (see Chapter 12, *Form in Music*). For our purposes here, the form could be very simple. For example, the melody could have four four bar phrases, two repeated eight-bar sections or two contrasting 16-bar sections.

3 Define the performance details.

Performance details such as dynamics and expression marks should be decided when you are working with the sounds of your instrument.

4 Visualise the performance.

Sometimes it is useful to imagine a performance of the completed composition. Think about the performers, the venue (where it is to be performed) and the audience. Define what it is you are trying to create.

This method of working helps you focus your efforts in a more structured way than method 1. You will have decided upon several elements before you actually start to experiment with sounds. For example, using method 2, you could decide to compose the following melody as described in Figure 2.1. While it is sometimes very helpful to have clear guidelines and ideas for composing like this, they should never restrict the creative process. You are the composer, and it is up to you to select, control and shape all the musical elements to achieve the sounds you want.

Title:	A Summer Day
Instrument:	Flute solo
Range:	Middle C upwards for 2 octaves (limit of performer)
Performer:	Me
Mood:	Relaxed, peaceful
Key:	D major
Style:	Modern, with a blues feel
Tempo:	Slow and leisurely
Time signature:	$\frac{4}{4}$
Rhythm:	No decision, although syncopation may be appropriate. The rhythm will be considered while working with the instrument.
Length:	16 bars (unless a longer piece develops)
Form:	Two 8-bar sections with repeats (unless a longer piece develops)
Effect:	To give the impression of a hot summer day

Remembering and recording your music

As it takes shape

As you are working on your melody or composition, trying out different possibilities, it is often helpful to note down your ideas as the music develops. This is a particularly useful practice if you have many different ideas, if the music is lengthy, or if you know that you will have to leave the composition in an unfinished state for a while. Choose a way of recording your work that is best suited to you. For example, you could write down the letter names of notes (D, E, F#, etc.), or notate the pitch and rhythm of your music on a stave. Tape recording is another useful way of storing your music or, if you are working with computer-linked equipment, you could save the music on disk.

The completed composition

Always record the completed composition and/or write out the music if you can. It is especially important to have a written or printed copy of the music if it is to be performed by someone else. Scores should always be as neat and accurate as possible, either handwritten (see Chapter 18) or printed with the aid of computer-linked equipment.

If the composition is to be submitted for an examination you should either write or print out your music, or include an annotation (a written explanation) of your taped music if you have not written a score.

Useful hints

The following list provides a summary of useful hints to help you compose a melody. Some of the suggestions are made for practical reasons, such as knowing the range of the instrument or voice for which you are composing. Other suggestions are based on examples of common practice, but should not restrict your own composition in any way if you do not feel that some of them are appropriate.

1 Know the range and limitations (if any) of the instrument or voice for which you are composing. Do not compose a tune which will be impossible to perform and also consider that the performer(s) may have limitations.

2 Think carefully about the mood, character and style of your melody and how you might achieve this.

3 Use an appropriate title.

4 Choose a key (or mode) that is appropriate for your music and suitable for the instrument and performer.

5 If your music has a tonality (rather than music which is atonal), establish the key at the beginning of the melody. The tonic note will often appear on the first beat of the music.

6 The shape of the melody should be appropriate and the intervals between adjacent melody notes carefully considered.

7 A melody may modulate or move to another key at some point, although it will nearly always end in the same key as it started. Melodies often end on the tonic note, which is frequently also a long note.

8 Melodic and rhythmic themes used in the first few bars are often repeated or developed, giving unity to the melody. Repeated ideas also add to the character, mood and style of the music.

9 A melody can be any length you choose. Many have a regular number of bars such as eight, 12, 16, 24, and 32 bars, often sub-divided into regular phrases.

10 Melodies can be extended with repeated whole sections, often four, eight or 16 bars in length.

11 Select an appropriate time signature and tempo for your melody.

12 The form or plan of the music is important. Repeated phrases or whole sections will contribute to the form, as will contrasting sections containing new, or complementary, material.

13 Performance details such as dynamics and expression marks can add much to your melody. Make sure that these are clearly indicated on any written score of the music.

14 Always work with real sounds when composing a melody. Listen critically, and be prepared to experiment with different ideas until you are satisfied with the results.

15 Keep a record of your work as the composition develops. It is useful to make rough jottings or a tape recording as you compose or save your music on disk.

16 Tape record and/or write out or print out your composition.

SUMMARY ASSIGNMENTS

1 Compose a melody using the procedure described as Method 1, beginning your work with no definite plan about the style, title, length, tempo, form of the melody, or the instrument or voice that will eventually play or sing it. Continue to work until the melody is finished and you are satisfied with the result. The choice of instrument or type of voice, performer and title, may be left until the melody is complete. Finally, record and/or notate your melody.

2 Compose one of the melodies suggested in Figure 2.2. Record and/or notate your composition.

Figure 2.2

	A	B	C
Title	The Highlander	Misty Mountain	Frenzy
Instrument	violin	clarinet	saxophone
Range	to suit performer	to suit performer	to suit performer
Performer	Your choice	Your choice	Your choice
Mood	bold and cheerful	sad, reflective	agitated
Key	A major	G minor	D minor
Style	dance-like	Impressionistic	Modern, jazzy
Tempo	Fairly quick	Slow	Fast
Time signature	$\frac{4}{4}$	$\frac{6}{8}$	$\frac{4}{4}$ or $\frac{5}{4}$
Rhythm	some dotted rhythms	Your choice	include rests
Length	16 bars	16 bars	16 or 24 bars
Form	two 8-bar sections	two 8-bar sections	Your choice

3 Compose a melody but select some, or all, of the following before you begin: title, instrument or voice, range, performer, mood, style, key (or mode), tempo, time signature, rhythm, length, form.

Record and notate the finished composition.

3
Repetition

Repetition is one of the most important compositional devices and appears in many guises. Either complete sections of the music may be repeated, or an entire melody, or any part of it, including phrases and musical figures may be imitated. One note, two notes sounded together, or even rhythmic phrases, may be repeated to provide the basis of a composition. Harmonies and chord sequences can also be repeated, making the repetition either exact or varied.

Repeats

As we have seen in Chapter 1, complete sections of music, or an entire melody can be repeated, not only extending the composition, but often providing the underlying structure, or form, of the whole piece. *The Hornpipe* from Handel's *Water Music,* shown on page 13 (Figure 1.11), provides such an example. In it, 16 bars of music are repeated to produce 96 bars in all. (More information about the structure and organisation of music can be found in chapter 12.) Another example of a melody containing repeated sections can be seen in Figure 3.1, a *Gavotte* from Bach's *Third English Suite* for keyboard. (Repeat signs are discussed on page 188.) This melody has two sections which repeat, clearly indicated by repeat signs.

J S Bach (1685–1750)

Gavotte II (or Musette) **from** *English Suite no. 3*   J S Bach   **Figure 3.1**

Some melodies have repeated phrases which are not repeated immediately after their first appearance. Additionally, the repeated phrase may also occur more than once. Some sections or phrases which are repeated could also be slightly changed on their subsequent appearance, as in Figure 3.2, the old English tune, *Portsmouth*.

Figure 3.2

Portsmouth   Traditional English tune

Refer to Figure 1.1, tune Z on page 6. The fine eight-bar melody which appears at the beginning of the song, *I know him so well*, is repeated but with different words, illustrating a highly effective use of repetition.

ASSIGNMENTS

1 Using music of your own choice, find four different examples which each contain repeated sections indicated by repeat signs.

2 Using music of your own choice, find four melodies which each use repeated melodic phrases but do not have repeat signs. The phrases may be repeated exactly, or slightly changed, on subsequent appearances.

3 Compose a 16-bar melody with repeated sections (such as two eight-bar sections, or a four-bar with a 12-bar section) for an instrument or voice of your own choice. Record, or write out, your melody. Give your composition a title.

Rhythmic repetition

Melodic repetition occurs where the pitch of some, or all, of the melody notes is repeated

The above musical examples contain rhythmic repetition, as well as illustrating melodic repetition. The repetition of a rhythm can be an important ingredient of a melody, providing balance and shape. For example, in the Bach *Gavotte*, the note values are crotchets and quavers, along with a few minims. The pattern of these note values, with its repeated rhythms, gives this melody its character. If you clap the rhythm of this gavotte, you will find many places where the rhythms are repeated or only slightly varied.

Another important aspect of rhythmic repetition may occur when there is more than one part to the music. Repeated rhythms, performed on untuned percussion instruments, can play an independent part, supporting or accompanying a melody. The repeated rhythm can provide the basis for a whole composition or improvisation (see Ostinato, page 34). A melody could be added to a repeated rhythm such as ♩ ♫♩ ♫ to create the passage:

ASSIGNMENTS

1 Find two melodies, each of 16 bars in length or longer, and comment on the use of rhythmic repetition in each. State which rhythm patterns occur most frequently and how, if at all, they are varied in the music.

2 Compose a 16-bar melody which features some rhythmic repetition. Give your composition a title and record and/or write down your melody.

3 Compose a melody in $\frac{4}{4}$ time with an accompanying repeated rhythm pattern. The melody should be 16 bars in length, with or without repeats, for an instrument of your choice. The rhythm pattern, for an untuned percussion instrument, should be one bar in length and repeated throughout your composition without changing. Give your composition a title and record and/or write down your music. (You could compose this music with the help of a friend, with one person playing the repeated rhythm and the other experimenting with the melody until you are satisfied with the result. If you are working on your own, you could record your repeated rhythm on tape or computer-linked equipment and then add the melody part.)

4 Maurice Ravel's *Bolero* provides an excellent example of rhythmic and melodic repetition. A side drum rhythm is repeated throughout, along with a melody which repeats many times with changing orchestration. Listen to *Bolero* and write brief notes about the music, commenting upon the effect of the repeated side drum rhythm and the way in which the melody is given to different instruments as the music gradually builds to its climax. Find a score of *Bolero* to see how the composer has organised the music for the orchestra.

Drones

Drone refers to a long, sustained sound and to the pipes of some instruments which sound a single, fixed note each, providing the accompaniment. The bagpipe's drone is an obvious example.

A drone consists of one or more notes, often sounding in the bass or lowest part (hence drone bass), sustained or persistently repeated throughout an entire piece, or part of it.

The musette was a French bagpipe of the seventeenth and eighteenth centuries. It gave its name to a dance-like piece with a pastoral character and a drone bass.

A drone bass contains only one note, sustained throughout an entire piece, or part of it. Examples occur in the **musette**, which often became a second gavotte in the eighteenth-century suite. The Bach *Gavotte II* in Figure 3.1, is really a musette, preceded in this keyboard suite by *Gavotte I*. The opening bars of the music are shown in full in Figure 3.3 with the bass line. The low G sounds throughout the first four repeated bars, and also through the remaining 12 bars, which are also repeated.

Figure 3.3   **Gavotte II (or Musette) from *English Suite no.3*   J S Bach

A drone can also contain two notes, frequently the tonic (the first note, or key-note of the major or minor scale), and the dominant (the fifth note of the scale), providing effective accompaniment to a melody. Figure 3.4 shows the tonic and the dominant two-note drone bass in an extract from *Highland Heather*.

Figure 3.4   ***Highland Heather***   C Binns

Pedal point

A pedal point is a sustained or repeated note, normally, although not always, in the bass or lowest part, above which there are changing and independent harmonies. When the pedal note occurs in an upper part, it is called an inverted pedal.

The pedal point (or pedal) is similar to the drone in that it is sustained or repeated. However, while the drone is often heard continuously throughout a composition, a pedal point may be any length and sometimes occurs only briefly. The note used as the pedal point is usually the tonic or dominant. It adds harmonic colour and can generate tension or excitement in the music. Pedal points are very useful for the composer and occur in a wide range of music, including contemporary pop music. A knowledge of harmony, or chords, will help in the use of the pedal point. Figures 3.5 and 3.6 provide examples of the pedal point.

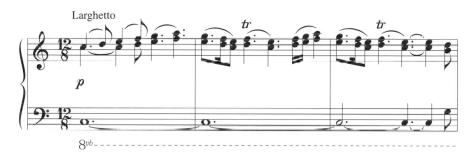

Pastoral Symphony from *Messiah*   G F Handel   **Figure 3.5**

Overture: Knightlife   C Binns   **Figure 3.6**

ASSIGNMENTS

1 Compose a melody of any suitable length with an accompanying drone. The drone may be one note or two notes sounded together throughout your composition and should be the lower or bass part. Each part may be performed together on one appropriate instrument such as piano, organ, electronic keyboard or bagpipe, or you may use two different instruments. Give your composition a title and record and/or write down your music.

2 Find two contrasting pieces of music which feature a pedal point. Write brief notes about them, commenting on the effect of each pedal point. State how the harmonies or chords in each piece change while the pedal note is sounded.

Ostinato

Ostinato literally means 'obstinate', and refers to a persistently repeated melodic phrase or rhythm in a composition. A melodic ostinato usually occurs in the same part at the same pitch.

The use of ostinato is found in many cultures and different types of music around the world. It features in Western classical music, in jazz and in pop music. Although melodic ostinato passages can occur in the upper voices, ostinato patterns are most frequently found in the bass, or lower part of the music (basso ostinato or ground bass) and provide the foundation for a composition. Many well-known compositions have been written featuring a ground bass ostinato. The rather solemn eight-bar ostinato from J. S. Bach's *Passacaglia in C minor* for organ is shown in Figure 3.7. It is repeated some twenty times as an exact repeat, or with some variation, to which the composer adds increasingly intricate melodic ideas.

Figure 3.7 *Passacaglia in C minor* J S Bach

In Figure 3.8, a ground bass provides the foundation for one of Purcell's most moving arias, Dido's lament, *When I am Laid in Earth* from the opera *Dido and Aeneas.* The voice sings a broad melody above the repeating instrumental bass line.

Figure 3.8 *When I am Laid in Earth* from *Dido and Aeneas* H Purcell

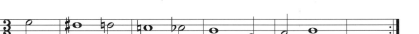

ASSIGNMENTS

1 Compose a simple bass ostinato which can be repeated many times and add your own melody to it. You could work on your own, perhaps using a tape recorder to play back your ostinato while you experiment with a melody. You could also work with a friend, one member of the team performing the ostinato, while the other improvises a contrasting melody at the same time. The melody and ostinato may be played on the same instrument, such as a piano or electronic keyboard, or you may choose two instruments. Vocal compositions featuring ostinato patterns can be very effective, so one or both parts may be sung. Give your composition a title and record and/or write down your music.

2 Select one of the ostinato patterns from Figure 3.9 and compose a vocal or instrumental melody to be performed with it. You may transpose your chosen ostinato to another key if you prefer. Work in the manner described in Assignment question 1, either on your own or with a partner. Give your composition a title and record and/or write down the finished composition.

Two ostinato patterns   *Figure 3.9*

3 Compose two different instrumental or vocal ostinato patterns which work well when performed together. Each ostinato can be a different length. When you are satisfied with your two ostinato patterns, compose a melody for instrument or voice which also fits with both of them. All three parts may start together, or may enter at different times. You could work on your own, using a tape recorder or computer-linked equipment, or you could work with two other partners, each playing a part in the music.

4 Listen to any piece of music which features an ostinato. Write brief notes about your choice, and comment on the number and type of instruments or voices used. Describe how the ostinato contributes to the music.

Sequence

Sequences are classified into two kinds. If a short phrase of the melody is immediately repeated at a higher or lower pitch, it is called a **melodic sequence**. If it is a series of chords, or harmonies, which is repeated at a higher or lower pitch it is called a **harmonic sequence.**

A sequence is the immediate repetition of a short musical phrase at a higher or lower pitch.

Examples of melodic and harmonic sequence.   *Figure 3.10*

Melodic sequence

Harmonic sequence

ASSIGNMENTS

1 Figure 3.11 is a composition for bass guitar. Write brief notes about the use of repetition and sequence in this piece.

Figure 3.11

The Fox   C Binns

2 Add your own melody to the music for bass guitar shown in Figure 3.11. You could compose a repeated 12-bar melody, or try a longer, improvised melody. Choose any suitable instrument or voice for your melody and record your finished composition.

3 Compose a melody which includes at least four sequences. The composition may be for any voice or instrument. Record and/or write down your completed melody.

4 Find examples of melodic sequence in two different pieces of music of your own choice. Write about each sequence and explain the effect which is created by their use in the melodies.

Imitation

When two or more melodies are combined simultaneously and each melody or voice has its own independent part, it is called counterpoint. It may be performed on a keyboard instrument or by groups of instruments or voices.

Imitation, which is an important feature of **counterpoint**, occurs when there are two or more voices or parts to the music and one of them enters with a phrase which is then copied by another voice or part. The imitative part may be at the same pitch, at the octave above or below, or at a different pitch. The first 12 bars of a keyboard piece by J S Bach, in Figure 3.12, opens with some imitation. The lower part begins two bars after the upper part, repeating the upper part's melody one octave lower. *Invention no 4 in D minor* also contains examples of sequence. If the imitation is of an entire part and copied exactly (either at the same pitch, or at a different pitch), then it becomes a **canon**. If the canon is written for voices, and each part follows at the same pitch successively repeating the canon, it is called a **round** or a perpetual canon. As the name implies, each singer in the round returns from the end of the melody to the beginning, repeating it as many times as appropriate. Well-known rounds and canons include *Three Blind Mice, London's Burning, Sumer is icumen in* and *Tallis's Canon*. You will find more information about rounds and canons in Chapter 13.

Invention no 4 in D minor   J S Bach   **Figure 3.12**

The most elaborate form of imitation occurs in the **fugue**. A short melody (called the subject) is stated at the beginning of the fugue in one voice and imitated by all the other parts (two, three, four or more) which enter successively. The subject then reappears throughout the fugue, stated by each of the different voices. The music moves through new keys before returning to the tonic key.

ASSIGNMENTS

Some knowledge of harmony or chords is useful when composing music which includes imitation. You may wish to leave the imitative part writing until you have studied later chapters. If you do not want to attempt question 1 at the moment, try questions 2 and 3 instead.

1 Compose a piece of music with two voices or parts showing some imitation. The music may be for a keyboard instrument, or for two other instruments. Record your completed composition.

2 Figure 3.13 is a short duet for two flutes, featuring examples of repetition, sequence and imitation. Discuss the use of these techniques in the piece, or write brief notes about them. If possible, perform the music.

3 Find some examples of imitation in one piece of music of your own choice. Write brief notes about the imitation and how it is used in the music you have chosen. If possible, perform the music, or listen to a recording of the piece.

Figure 3.13

Bel Air (Duet for flutes)

C Binns

SUMMARY ASSIGNMENTS

1 Compose some music which includes some of the following:
repeats, melodic and/or rhythmic repetition, drone, pedal point, ostinato, sequence, imitation.

Your music may be for any number of appropriate voices or instruments. If possible, write down your finished composition or provide an annotation (explanatory notes) about your work. Perform and record the composition.

2 The work of J. S. Bach has endless examples of many of the techniques described in this chapter. Study the score of any one composition by J. S. Bach, and listen to a recording of the music. Then, write about any points of interest you have found, particularly if they include the techniques explained in this chapter. If you are unsure which piece to select, you could start by choosing from the *Well-Tempered Clavier* (sometimes called the *Forty-Eight*), which contains an assortment of preludes and fugues; forty-eight to be precise!

4

Modulation and embellishments

A change from one key to another in a composition is called modulation.

As we have seen in Chapter 1, it is important to consider carefully the key of your music, how the key is established, and whether the key is to change. Many tunes contain one or more modulations. Once in a new key, the music may remain there for some time, return immediately to the original key, or modulate again to yet another key. Usually, the music returns to the original key by the end of the piece. The melody in Figure 4.1 is in the key of B♭ major, which briefly modulates to the key of F major before returning to the original key. Other examples of melodies which include a modulation are tunes I, L, O, Q and R, of Figure 1.1.

Figure 4.1 An example of modulation

The most common modulations are to **related keys** such as the **relative minor**, the **relative major**, the **dominant** or **subdominant** and their relative minor or major keys. To understand the terms relative major and relative minor you need to be familiar with key signatures. Each major scale shares a key signature with a minor scale, its relative minor; and each minor scale shares a key signature with a major scale, its relative major. For example, the relative minor of G major is E minor, and the relative major of E minor is G major. Both keys share the same **key signature**, namely, one sharp.

The **dominant** key is the key built upon the fifth degree of the original scale. For example, if the original key is G major, the dominant key is D major. The **subdominant** key is built upon the fourth degree of the original scale. For example, if the original key is G major, the subdominant key is C major. Each of these new (major) keys will also have a relative minor key. The relative minor key of D major is B minor and, in relation to

the original key of G major, is called the **dominant relative minor** key.
The relative minor key of C major is A minor and, in relation to the
original key of G major, is called the **subdominant relative minor** key.
More information about major and minor keys can be found in the
Rudiments and Reference section.

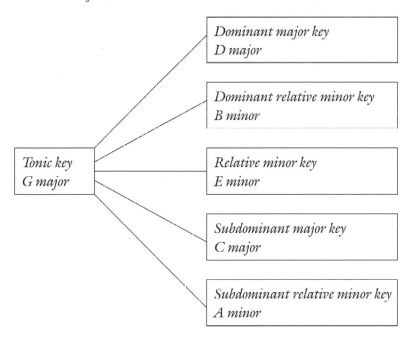

*Figure 4.2 Some of the keys
to which a composition in
G major could modulate.*

All the new keys in Figure 4.2 contain many of the notes of the original
key, and modulation is effected by the introduction of the new note(s).
Moving from G major to D major, for instance, requires the introduction
of the note C#, although the new note does not necessarily have to appear
in the melody. The new note may occur in the supporting harmony.

*Figure 4.3 Three melodies
which modulate*

When harmonies or chords are also used (instead of just a melody), a
modulation can be prepared by using notes of a chord, common to both
the original and the new key. For example, if chords were to be added to
the previous melody which modulates from G major to D major, a chord
common to both keys is E minor, and could be introduced as in Figure 4.4

Figure 4.4 A modulation from G major to D major

To understand this kind of modulation, some information about scales, and harmony or chords, is required.

Whole sections of a composition may be in a new key and this can be very effective. When the new key is established, new musical material may be introduced, or the original melody and harmony may be repeated, sometimes exactly note-for-note, but transposed into the new key. Examples can be found in a wide variety of music. Listen to, and look at Schubert's *Hörch, hörch! die Lerch (Hark, Hark! the Lark)*, for example.

Part of the *Theme from Lovejoy* in Figure 4.5 illustrates a very effective use of modulation. The first six bars of the melody in G major are repeated, and then the theme moves to the key of B♭ major, returning at the end of eight bars to the home key of G major. Elements of the opening theme are restated in the new key.

Figure 4.5   ***Theme from Lovejoy***   Dennis King

ASSIGNMENTS

1 Compose a melody of eight or 16 bars which includes one modulation. Give your melody a title and choose a suitable instrument or voice to perform it. Either record or write down your composition.

2 Select a piece of music to perform which includes at least one modulation. The music can be a solo or for a group of performers. If possible (perhaps as part of your classroom work), perform the music to a group of friends. Introduce your

performance by stating the title, composer and key of the music. Explain
where the modulations occur and identify the keys to which the music travels.

3 Study the music and listen to a recording of any one of Schubert's songs which
includes some modulation. Write a few notes about the use of modulation in
the song and any other points of interest, such as the words, mood, range, key,
length, tempo and other performance details.

4 Find an example of a pop song that includes some modulation or has an entire
section performed in a new key. Write brief details about the song, describing
the modulation. Mention any other points of interest such as the words, mood,
range, key, length, tempo and other performance details.

Embellishments

In music, embellishments can be introduced into compositions and
performances to give added interest and to make the music more elaborate.
Embellishments are found in the music of many cultures. For example, in
Western European music, during the Baroque period, the age of J S Bach
(1685–1750) and G F Handel (1685–1759), it was customary for
performers to improvise and expand upon the written music by adding
their own embellishments. As a composer, you will have to decide whether
to use embellishments in your music, or whether you require the
performers to add their own embellishments.

These embellishments include the use of **unessential notes** and
ornaments. Unessential notes (sometimes referred to as **non-harmony
notes**, or **non-harmonic notes**) are notes occurring in the melody, or any
other part (for example, the bass part), which do not belong to the chord
being sounded at that point in the music. Some types of unessential notes
are very simple, one-note additions to the music, but their use can be very
effective. Here, **passing notes**, **auxiliary notes**, and **notes of anticipation**
are explained. There are rules governing their use in formal harmony, but
this should not deter you from experimenting with unessential notes in
your own compositions.

A **passing note** moves by step between two harmony notes, often the
interval of a third apart (although a **chromatic passing note** may occur
between two harmony notes the interval of a major 2nd apart). The two
harmony notes may belong to the same chord (example *a*) or two different
chords (example *b*). The chords here are identified by letters placed above
the music and by Roman numerals (see page 53) written underneath.

The word *embellish* means
'to beautify' or 'to make
more interesting by adding
detail'.

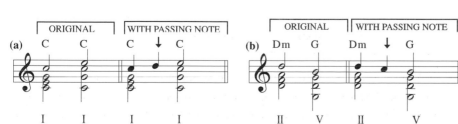

*Figure 4.6 Passing notes,
auxiliary notes and notes of
anticipation*

An **auxiliary note** follows a harmony note, moving by step above (called an **upper auxiliary note**) or below (a **lower auxiliary note**), and then returning to the same harmony note.

A note of **anticipation** belongs to the chord which follows it, but sounded before the chord occurs. Anticipations most commonly occur at **cadences** (see page 60).

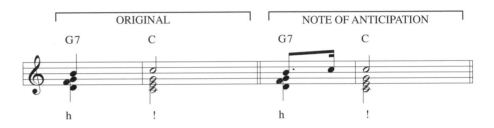

Figure 4.7 is a melody to which some unessential notes have been added:

Figure 4.7   ORIGINAL:

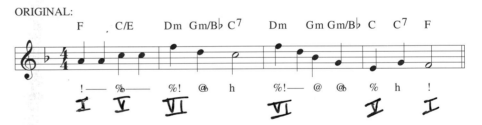

WITH UNESSENTIAL NOTES:

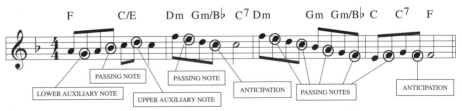

Further embellishments can be achieved by using ornaments. These include the **trill, turn, appoggiatura, acciaccatura** and the **mordent**. More information on these ornaments can be found in the *Rudiments and Reference* section of the book.

Ornaments can add character and elaboration to many styles of music, but must be added with care and economy! Don't introduce too many into the music, and always think about the abilities of the performers. In a written score of your music, you can choose whether or not to write out the

ornaments, or to indicate them by writing the appropriate sign over the
music. In Figure 4.8, a trill has been added to the first melody, and an upper
and lower mordent have been added to the second melody. Figure 4.9 is
from a longer composition for solo violin featuring many ornaments and
embellishments. This extract includes acciaccaturas, mordents and turns.

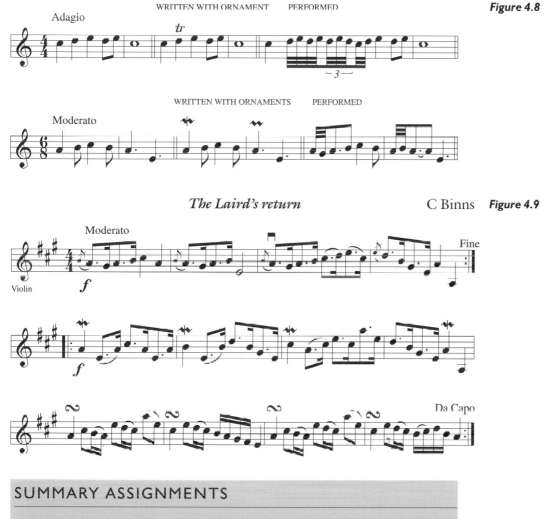

Figure 4.8

The Laird's return   C Binns   Figure 4.9

SUMMARY ASSIGNMENTS

1 Compose a melody in any style that you like and include some ornaments.
Give your composition a suitable title and record and write down your
composition.

2 Take a simple melody, such as a folk song, which does not have any ornaments
indicated on the score and add ornaments of your choice to the music. Do not
include any ornament which is not appropriate or playable. Perform the two
versions of the melody (one without ornaments and one with ornaments) and
compare the effect each has. Do you prefer the melody without
ornamentation or with it?

3 Find one piece of music which has some ornaments indicated on the score.
Write about the different ornaments in the music and explain how each should
be performed. If possible, perform the music yourself, playing all the
ornaments.

5
Composing a song

The first steps

Having studied in the previous chapters what makes a good melody, and the importance of repetition, embellishments and ornaments, we shall now consider how to combine words and music to compose a song. For the moment, let us assume that you have chosen your words, and that you are going to set the words to music. There follows a list of suggestions to help you compose your song:

1 Read the words through several times and try to understand the meaning and mood of them.

2 The words may suggest a natural rhythm to you as you say them aloud. You should then be able to write accents over the important words or syllables that are to be stressed. For example:

>   >   >   >
The lion and the unicorn were fighting for the crown.

When you set the words to music, the important words and syllables will fall on the first beat, or a strong beat, of a bar.

3 Think about the rhythm suggested by the words and decide upon a suitable time signature. For the moment, use only one note for each syllable:

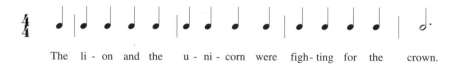

The li - on and the u - ni - corn were figh- ting for the crown.

4 Experiment with the rhythm until it is exactly what you want:

The li - on and the u - ni - corn were figh- ting for the crown.

5 Add a melody to fit the words and rhythm. Consider:
- **The melody**. Be familiar with the principles of melody writing as outlined in the previous chapters. This will help you to produce an effective melody which has shape and character.
- **Type of voice**. Decide upon the type of voice or voices that will perform your song.
- **Range and key**. The vocal part must be pitched within a suitable range, in an appropriate key, and must be 'singable'.
- **Mood**. The music should reflect and emphasise the mood of the words. Use your imagination.
- **Tempo**. Choose an appropriate speed.

Be critical. Work on your song, singing it, or playing it on an instrument, until you are quite satisfied with the result.

6 If you write out your song, you should put a suitable clef, a key signature and a time signature. Add the words underneath the melody, making it clear which word or syllable fits each note.

7 Indicate the tempo, and add dynamics and phrasing.

8 For the moment, we have concentrated on composing a melody with words, but without accompaniment. You may also wish to add an accompaniment or chords to your song. This aspect is dealt with in Chapter 6, *Chords*. To complete the example below, chords for guitar or a keyboard instrument have been added.

Accented words

It is possible to stress any syllable or word when writing a song. You should, however, emphasise those words which you think are important. In Figure 5.1, the same words have been set to four different rhythms. Any one of the four settings is appropriate.

Figure 5.1 **Rhythms**

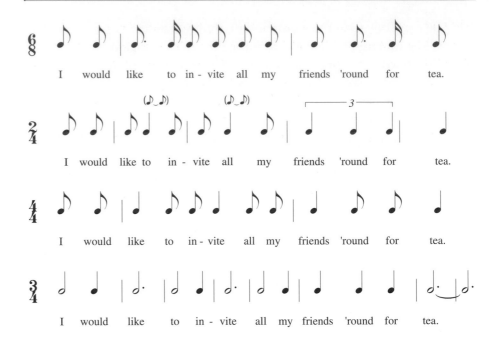

Key

Your choice of key is very important. You should consider whether or not your song will be composed in a major or minor key. In Figure 5.2, for example, the words *I would like to invite all my friends 'round for tea* are set in the key of F major and F minor. Sing or play these melodies, taking care to observe the key signature of each piece.

Figure 5.2

While the two melodies differ only in the pitch of one note which occurs three times (the version in F major has three As, while the version in F minor has three A♭s), the effect upon the mood is considerable. In the key of F major, the song is bright and quite jolly. In the key of F minor, the mood is rather sad and mournful. The mood is also reinforced if an appropriate tempo is added.

You should also consider which key best suits the range of the voice which you have chosen. For example, if your melody has a range of ten notes, then you should ensure that the upper and lower extremes of the melody's range are within the range, or compass, of your singer's voice. If the music was intended for soprano voice, then the key of D major would accommodate a ten-note range from D to F #. In the key of G major, however, the range of the song would either be too low, or perhaps a little too high.

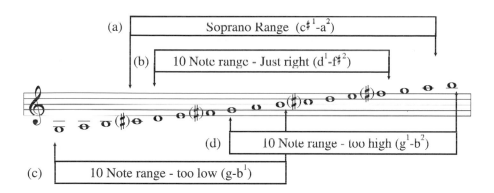

Figure 5.3 Range

If your song is to be accompanied, you should consider which key would also be suitable for the instrument, or instruments, which you have chosen. For example, vocal music in the key of G♭ major may present no problem to the singer, but could prove difficult to some pianists.

One note, one syllable?

It is customary in vocal music to write individual note values for each syllable. The rules for grouping of notes do not normally apply. Only when two or more notes represent one word or syllable do we join notes together with a slur or phrase mark.

Figure 5.4 One note, one syllable?

In many songs, as in the examples shown, one note is allocated for each word or syllable.

However, you may find that in more recent music, for example some pop songs, this custom is not followed, and that the melody of the song has notes grouped as we would normally write them. Two vocal melodies shown in Figure 1.1, illustrate these two approaches. Compare Tune Q, *Why do the Nations?* with Tune Z, *I know him so well*. Both methods are acceptable.

There may be many instances when you want to write more than one note for a single word or syllable. Figure 5.5, taken from Handel's *Messiah*, illustrates what can be done with the word *amen*.

Figure 5.5   Extracts from *Amen* from *Messiah*   G F Handel

Word-painting

In word-painting, the music expresses the idea or mood of a particular word or phrase.

It is important that the words and music of your song complement each other. Usually, sad words require sad music, and happy words demand happy music. Sometimes, lyrics may reflect more than one mood, and moods may change within a song. Some composers have chosen to emphasise certain words by using word-painting.

Word-painting was widely used in the Renaissance and Baroque periods. It can be found in many of the madrigals of the second half of the sixteenth century, and later in the vocal work of G F Handel and J S Bach. Categories of words suitable for this treatment have been suggested and include emotions (rejoice, rage, sorrow, weep), motion (turned, ascending, risen), places (heaven, mountain, valley), time (quickly) and number (twice). Such words could all be given a special musical significance. Figure 5.6 from Handel's *Messiah* illustrates the composer's use of word painting.

Figure 5.6   **Extracts from *Every valley shall be exalted* from *Messiah*** G F Handel

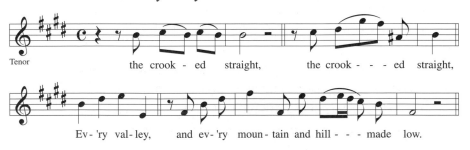

Methods of working

In Chapter 2, approaches to the process of composition were shown. These approaches are quite valid when composing a song. In addition, when composing a song you must decide whether or not to write your own words, or use somebody else's. If you are using your own words you must choose whether to write the words first and add the melody, or compose the melody and write some words to fit the tune.

Whichever way you choose to work, adding a melody to words, or adding words to your melody, you may like to develop your ideas by improvising, or experimenting, on an instrument or with your voice.

Many musicians compose their songs by improvising on a keyboard or guitar as the song gradually takes shape. If you do not want to write out your song as you are working on it, you can always record your efforts, or transcribe (write out) the song later from the tape, or ask someone to help you. If you are working with a pop group or other musicians it may be sufficient just to sing or play the song to them or hand out a copy of the words with chords added over the appropriate words.

Many guitarists and drummers enjoy working this way and will be able to cope with this approach, playing along and improvising their own parts. It is a good idea to record the results and then carefully listen to each contribution to make sure it is just what you want. Working in this way can produce exciting results as a group composition rather than as an individual one. Incidentally, if you are going to submit work of this nature for an examination be sure that you know exactly who has contributed what!

SUMMARY ASSIGNMENTS

1 Study the score of Handel's *Messiah* and find examples of word-painting. List ten different examples from this oratorio, and write about each one, describing the way in which Handel has used word-painting.

2 Choose one English madrigal and comment on its use of word painting. Write brief notes about your findings and give examples to support your answer.

3 Find one song of your choice which, in your opinion, has successfully combined an appropriate melody with the words. Explain how this is achieved, mentioning the mood and key of the song, the tempo and any other points of interest.

4 Select a phrase or sentence and compose two different short melodies to fit the same set of words. For example, you may choose a major and a minor key, or two different time signatures and rhythms to provide a contrast between your two versions.

Either write out your two brief melodies, placing each word or syllable under the correct note, or perform your songs and record them

5 Compose a melody to fit one of the sets of words in Figure 5.7. Words, phrases and entire lines in the poems may be repeated to emphasise the meaning and to extend the melody if required. Write down or record the completed song.

Figure 5.7 Three poems

Birds' nests   Anon

The skylark's nest among the
grass
And waving corn Is found;
The robin's on a shady bank,
With oak leaves strewn around.

Arise! Chill Vard   Anon

Arise! Chill Vard, from the ice
bound depths,
And greet the morning sun.
Victorious now, thy fate awaits,
Your final battle won.

Street boy   Gareth Owen

Just you look at me, man,
Stompin' down the street
My crombie stuffed with biceps
My boots is filled with feet.

Just you hark to me, man,
When they call us out
My head is full of silence
My mouth is full of shout.

Just you watch me move, man.
Steady like a clock
My heart is spaced on blue beat
My soul is stoned on rock.

Just you read my name, man,
Writ for all to see
The walls is red with stories
The streets is filled with me.

6 Compose a song with words which are not your own. Record and write down your completed composition.

7 Compose a song using words that you have written. Record and write down your completed composition.

6
Chords

Chords are extremely useful to the composer, and a knowledge of them can help you in many aspects of your own work. For example, chords can be used to help compose a melody or an accompaniment, and patterns of chords can provide the basis, or form, of an entire composition.

Triads

A chord containing three notes is called a **triad**. It will contain a **root** (the note the chord is built upon and named after), with notes the interval of a **3rd** and a **5th** above it. A triad may be built upon any of the notes, or degrees, of any major or minor scale. (For information about intervals and degrees of the scale, see the *Rudiments and Reference* section). Here, triads have been written upon the notes of the scale of C major:

A chord is a group of three or more notes sounded together.

When writing a triad, notice that if the root of a triad is written on a line, then all the notes of that triad are written on lines. If the root of the triad is written in a space, then all the notes of that triad are written in spaces. A triad takes its name from the **degree of the scale** upon which it is built, such as the tonic triad or the subdominant triad. Triads can also be identified by Roman numerals:

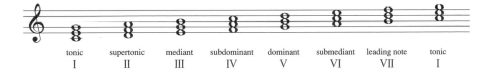

tonic	supertonic	mediant	subdominant	dominant	submediant	leading note	tonic
I	II	III	IV	V	VI	VII	I

Triads and chords are described as **major, minor, diminished** or **augmented**.

Figure 6.1 Types of triads

a *major triad* consists of a major 3rd and a perfect 5th.

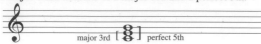

a *minor triad* consists of a minor 3rd and a perfect 5th.

an *augmented triad* consists of a major 3rd and an augmented 5th.

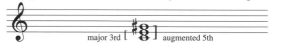

a *diminished triad* consists of a minor 3rd and an diminished 5th.

The triads shown on page 53 have all been built upon the degrees of the scale, with the lowest note of each triad as the root. The notes in a triad do not have to be arranged in **root position**, and may appear in **inversion**. This means that instead of the root being the lowest note of the triad, the 3rd or the 5th note can be the lowest.

tonic triad
in root position,
C major

tonic triad
in first inversion,
C major

tonic triad
in second inversion,
C major

In addition to the Roman numerals which appear under triads, the letters **b** and **c** are used to signify inversions. A first inversion is indicated by the letter **b**, and a second inversion by the letter **c**.

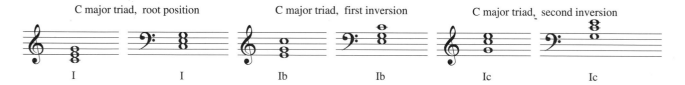

When the notes of a triad are as close together as possible, the triad is described as being in **close position**.

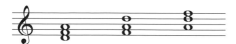

When the notes of a triad are more widely spaced and not arranged together as closely as possible, the triad is described as being in **open position**.

Do not confuse the numbers which describe **the intervals between the lowest note and the two upper notes of a triad** (the interval of a 3rd and a 5th above the root) with the numbers which represent **the degrees of a scale** (such as the third degree of the scale, or the fifth degree of the scale). For example, this is a triad built upon the second degree of the scale of C major. It is a minor triad, and is called the **supertonic triad**:

The triad contains a root (D), and above it, the interval of a 3rd (F), and the interval of a 5th (A). The terms **3rd** and **5th** refer to the intervals between the upper notes and the root of the triad, and not to the degrees of the scale. The third degree of the scale is the note E, and the fifth degree is G, neither of which has any connection with this triad.

A triad built upon a particular degree of a scale can appear in another scale with the same notes but with a different name. For example, a triad built upon the tonic note of the scale of C major includes the notes C-E-G. It is referred to as the **tonic** triad. However, a triad with the same notes (C-E-G) also occurs in the scale of G major, but here it is the triad built upon the fourth degree of the scale and is called the **subdominant** triad. The same triad also appears on the fifth degree of the scale of F major and is called the **dominant** triad.

Figure 6.2 Triads

Chords

When the notes of a triad or chord are played separately, in succession, instead of all together, it is called a broken chord

Chords may contain more than three notes. Often, the additional notes will just be repeated notes of the triad, but written and sounded at a different pitch. For example, the tonic triad of C major with notes C-E-G, could appear as a five-note chord containing C-C-C-E-G. All the following are examples of the chord of C major:

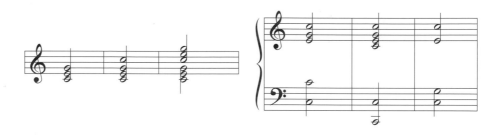

Figure 6.3 shows various ways of presenting and extending a simple triad of C major (C-E-G).

Figure 6.3

Combining chords

The basis of a composition can be formed by combining several chords into a **chord progression** or **chord sequence**. A simple example could use the notes of the tonic triad of C major (C-E-G) and notes of the dominant triad in the same key (G-B-D). These notes could be presented in many ways, as shown in Figure 6.4.

Figure 6.4

You may choose any triads or chords for your composition. One approach is to use a selection of any triads or chords built upon the scale of the key that you are working in. For example, triads built upon the notes of the scale of G major look like this:

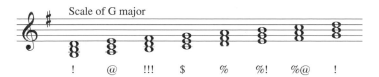

In the first version of Figure 6.5, three of the above triads have been used: the **tonic** (G major or chord I), **subdominant** (C major or chord IV) and **dominant** (D major or chord V). The three triads I, IV and V are called the **primary triads.** The left-hand accompaniment consists of broken chords. This arpeggio use of the notes in the bass or left hand is called an **Alberti Bass** and is commonly found in keyboard music.

Figure 6.5(i)   *Catherine and Claire (first version)*   C Binns

In the first version, only the notes found in each chord have been used. To develop this music further, you could work on the melody, perhaps at the keyboard, adding other notes, or embellishments. So the opening phrase:

could become:

The composition could be further extended by repeating all or part of the eight bars already composed, or by extending and developing some of the melodic or rhythmic ideas. A further eight bars could be added using some new chords, or by using the same ideas, but moving into a minor key, such as the relative E minor. Version two of Figure 6.5 demonstrates this.

Figure 6.5(ii) *Catherine and Claire (second version)* C Binns

Figure 6.6 Three pieces of music featuring broken chords

Sonatina in G Op. 36, no.5 M Clementi

Here is the opening of a sonatina by M Clementi (1752 - 1832). Can you see how the composer has used broken chords for the left hand?

This sonata by W A Mozart (1756–1791) also features broken chords for the left hand.

First movement from Sonata in C, K 545   W A Mozart

First movement from Sonata Op. 27 no. 2   L van Beethoven

An extract from the first movement of the 'Moonlight' Sonata by L.van Beethoven (1770-1827), which is built upon broken chords played by the right hand, with long sustained notes in the left hand.

ASSIGNMENTS

1 Compose a piece of music for piano or a keyboard instrument, built upon three or four different chords. You may use broken chords if you wish, and your composition may be in any style. Try writing out your music using two bracketed staves with a treble and bass clef. Give the composition an appropriate title, indicating tempo and adding dynamic marks. If you do not want to write out the music, perform and record the piece.

2 Find a piece of music in any style written for piano or a keyboard instrument which features broken chords. Write about how the composer has used broken chords. Identify some of the chords which have been used and comment on the melody.

Cadences

A cadence occurs at the end of a composition, a section or phrase. It brings the music to a point of rest, to a breathing place or to a conclusion. If chords are added to a melody, those occurring at the end of phrases or sections, enhance and give character to the cadences. There are four types of cadence most frequently used, and each is identified by a progression of two particular chords .

Cadences ending on the tonic chord have an air of finality about them. They include the **perfect cadence** and the **plagal cadence**. The perfect cadence, dominant chord (V) to tonic chord (I) sounds final and complete. The plagal cadence, subdominant chord (IV) to tonic chord (I), also sounds final, and may remind you of 'Amen'.

Figure 6.7 Four types of cadences

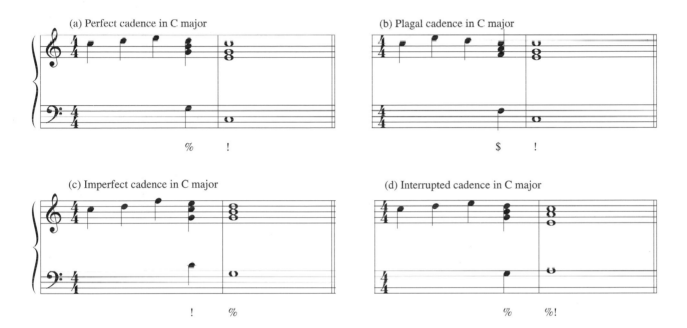

Cadences which do not end on the tonic chord sound unfinished. They include the **imperfect** and the **interrupted** cadences. The imperfect cadence, tonic chord (I), or any other chord, to dominant chord (V), sounds unfinished and incomplete. It suggests that more music will follow the cadence. The interrupted cadence, dominant chord (V) to any chord except the tonic (I), also sounds unfinished and incomplete. The listener anticipates that the dominant (V) will be followed by the tonic chord (I), but the music is 'interrupted' as a chord other than the tonic is used, frequently the submediant (VI). In your own compositions, always think carefully about cadences, and the effect that each creates.

More chord sequences

Any number of chords may be combined to produce a chord sequence. Figure 6.8 provides some examples. Each chord sequence may be repeated, extended or combined with other sequences to provide the basis for a composition.

The chord sequence for a pop song is shown in Figure 6.9. Although a stave with pitch and rhythms is not used, the chord sequence written like this provides sufficient information for the guitar, bass guitar and keyboard to perform their parts.

Figure 6.8 A selection of chord sequences.

A selection of chord sequences.

Each chord can last for as many beats or bars as you wish. The chord numbers will help you to play the sequences in any key.

C	G	F	G		I	V	IV	V
C	G	F	C		I	V	IV	I
C	F	C	G		I	IV	I	V
C	F	Em	Dm		I	IV	III	II
C	Am	Dm	G		I	VI	II	V
C	Am	F	G		I	VI	IV	V
C	Em	F	G		I	III	IV	V
C	Em	Dm	G		I	III	II	V
C	Dm	C	G		I	II	I	V
C	Dm	Em	F		I	II	III	IV
C	Dm	F	G		I	II	IV	V
C	B♭	C	B♭		I	♭VII	I	♭VII
C	B♭	A♭	G		I	♭VII	♭VI	V
C	E♭	F	G		I	♭III	IV	V
C	E♭	B♭	G		I	♭III	♭VII	V

C	F	C	G	F	C				I	IV	I	V	IV	I		
C	G	Am	Em	F	C	C	G		I	V	VI	III	IV	I	I	V
C	C	F	C	G	F	C	G		I	I	IV	I	V	IV	I	V

The flat sign (♭) placed in front of a chord number means that the chord is built upon the flattened degree of the scale.

For example, in the scale of C major, VII means a chord built upon the note B, the seventh degree of that scale. The notes of the chord are B, D and F.

♭VII in the scale of C major means a chord built upon the note B♭, the flattened seventh of that scale. The notes of the chord are B♭, D and F.

Figure 6.9   **Chord sequence for *Bop Shawaddy Wap***   C Binns

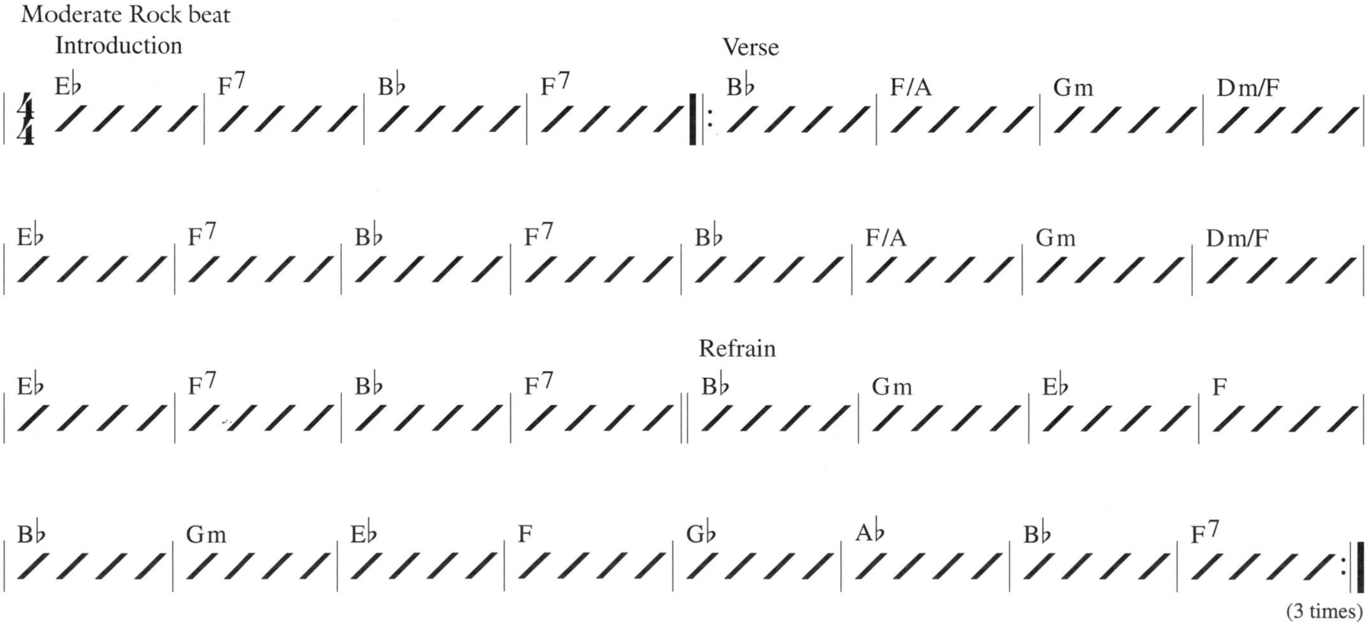

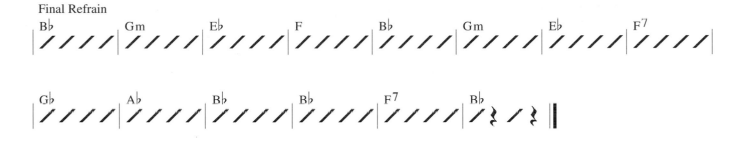

Final Refrain

ASSIGNMENTS

1 Choose one of the chord sequences given on page 62 as the basis for your own piece of music. You may repeat the chord sequence, add to it, or combine it with another chord sequence to produce your music if you wish. Record and write out your completed composition.

2 Working with a friend, choose a chord sequence to use as the basis for a composition. One person can perform the chord sequence on a suitable instrument, while the other tries out ideas for a melody, improvising or experimenting on an instrument or with the voice. Continue working in this way until you have a completed composition and you are quite satisfied with the results. Record and write down your composition, carefully noting the contribution to the music made by each person.

A choice of chords

While many chord sequences use chords that are built upon notes of a scale in one particular key, it is possible to choose chords of any description, from any key, to use in your compositions. The outcome of combining

Name of major chord	Notes in chord	Name of minor chord	Notes in chord
C major	C E G	C minor	C E♭ G
C♯ major	C♯ E♯ G♯	C♯ minor	C♯ E G♯
D♭ major	D♭ F A♭	D♭ minor	D♭ F♭ A♭
D major	D F♯ A	D minor	D F A
E♭ major	E♭ G B♭	E♭ minor	E♭ G♭ B♭
E major	E G♯ B	E minor	E G B
F major	F A C	F minor	F A♭ C
F♯ major	F♯ A♯ C♯	F♯ minor	F♯ A C♯
G♭ major	G♭ B♭ D♭	G♭ minor	G♭ B♭♭ D♭
G major	G B D	G minor	G B♭ D
G♯ major	G♯ B♯ D♯	G♯ minor	G♯ B D♯
A♭ major	A♭ C E♭	A♭ minor	A♭ C♭ E♭
A major	A C♯ E	A minor	A C E
B♭ major	B♭ D F	B♭ minor	B♭ D♭ F
B major	B D♯ F♯	B minor	B D F♯

Figure 6.10 *Some major and minor chords. Notes which sound the same, but are named and written differently (e.g. F♯ and G♭) according to the key in which they occur, are called* **enharmonic.**

chords which are not closely related can produce some exciting results. Figure 6.10 shows a list of some major and minor chords which could be used in your compositions.

ASSIGNMENT

Choose several chords from Figure 6.10 and experiment with them on a keyboard instrument, combining your chosen chords to use as the basis for a composition. You may wish to present the chords as broken chords, repeat one or more chords in rhythmic phrases, or add a melody to the chords. Record the finished result and write a brief annotation to describe what you have done.

Melody with chords

Some instrumentalists, such as guitarists and keyboard players, can read and perform music which is written as a melody with chords indicated by letters and numbers (called chord symbols) added above or below the music. Much popular music is written out in this manner, or as a melody on one stave, with piano (or keyboard) accompaniment on two additional staves. There are two methods of working to produce a melody with chords. Either compose a melody and then fit chords to it, or find some chords or a chord sequence which you like and add a melody to it.

Figure 6.11 is an example of a melody for electric guitar, with added chords for rhythm guitar and keyboard. Bass guitar can play the note suggested by the chord and improvise around the chords given, and drums can provide a strong rhythm.

Figure 6.11   *Pig in the middle*   C Binns

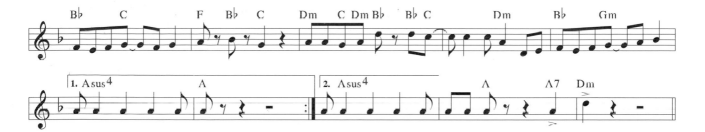

ASSIGNMENT

Compose a melody complete with chords and, if possible, write down and record your composition. You may choose to compose the melody first and then add chords to it, or you may prefer to work on a chord sequence first and then add the melody to the chords.

More advanced chords

Chords can be made more elaborate by the addition of an extra note, or notes, to the three notes (root, 3rd, 5th) of a triad. The extra note is indicated by a number written next to the chord letter, such as C^6 or $C\,min^7$. The number given in a chord symbol always indicates the interval between the root of the chord and the added note. So, C^6 for example, contains the root, 3rd, and 5th plus a 6th, making it C-E-G-A. The exact grouping or inversion of the chord is often left to the discretion of the performer. Figure 6.12 is a list of the more common additions to chords including the chord symbol or notation for each. The examples given are all variations of a chord of C.

Chord Symbol	Interpretation of Chord Symbol	Notes in the Chord
C	C major	C E G
Cm or C min	C minor	C E♭ G
C dim or C°	C diminished	C E♭ G♭
C aug or C+	C augmented	C E G♯
C sus 4 or C sus	C major with added 4th (but without a 3rd)	C F G
C^6	C major with added 6th	C E G A
C^7	C major with minor (flattened) 7th	C E G B♭
$C\,maj^7$	C major with major 7th	C E G B
$C\,min^7$	C minor with minor (flattened) 7th	C E♭ G B♭
C^9	C major with minor (flattened) 7th and added 9th	C E G B♭ D
$Cm^{7♭5}$ or Cm^{7-5}	C minor with minor 7th and flattened 5th	C E♭ G♭ B♭
C/E or C(E bass)	C major with the note E in the bass (i.e. in first inversion)	C E G (with E on the bass)

Figure 6.12

SUMMARY ASSIGNMENTS

1 Find a copy of some music which has chord symbols written above (or below) the melody. Choose six different chords from this music and list the notes which belong to each chord. For example, C7 = C, E, G, B♭.

2 Figure 6.13 is a composition for oboe and piano using a variety of chords. The oboe plays the melody while the piano improvises an accompaniment based upon the given chords.

Try to work out the notes in each chord and perform the composition with a friend, or ask your teacher to play it for you. If you do not have a piano or an oboe, the music may be performed on any suitable instruments such as violin and electronic keyboard, or flute and guitar. You will have to transpose one of the parts if you decide that the solo is to be performed by a transposing instrument .

Figure 6.13   *Another Blue Day*   C Binns

7
Accompaniment

Some songs are intended to be sung unaccompanied, but most require instrumental or vocal accompaniment. Many songs are written with an accompanying piano part and, more recently, with chords indicated above the music (by chord symbols). Pop music is seldom written out as a full score with individual parts. The copy available in shops will usually have a melody line with piano/keyboard accompaniment like this:

Figure 7.1   *Please don't change* from *School Rules*   C Binns

Piano or keyboard accompaniment

Some piano accompaniments are quite simple, providing background and support to a solo melody. Other accompaniments will have a greater independence and, musically, will be as interesting and as important as the melody itself. Whatever style you choose, a good accompaniment will add much to your melody. A knowledge of chords will help you to compose a piano or keyboard accompaniment. A step-by-step guide to help you compose an accompaniment follows:

1 Compose your melody.

There are many approaches to composing a melody and a knowledge of chords can be very useful. The following four-bar melody for recorder was composed by first choosing a chord sequence (F major, B♭ major, F major, C major) and then using some or all of the notes from each chord in the melody. For example, the chord of F major (F-A-C) suggested notes for bars 1 and 3, and the notes in the chord of B♭ major (B♭-D-F) suggested notes for bar 2.

2 Choose suitable chords to accompany your melody.

If you have composed your melody by first choosing chords (as shown in Step 1 above) proceed now to Step 3. If you have composed your melody without reference to chords, you will now need to experiment (probably on a keyboard instrument or guitar), trying out different chords as you play or sing the melody. Add one or two chords to each bar of melody and listen carefully to the effect. Do not worry too much about the style of the accompaniment at this stage. Make a note of your choice of chords, like this:

3 Experiment with your chords.

Try your chosen chords in a variety of inversions and in different positions on the keyboard, re-arranging the notes until you are satisfied with the sounds. The left-hand chords in example **3a** below, move awkwardly, and are not always written in the most suitable position, while the chords in example **3b** are a little easier to play and sound quite satisfactory.

4 Decide upon the style of the accompaniment.

You may know the style of accompaniment which you want as soon as
you begin to compose your melody. Or, as you try out ideas on the
keyboard, the accompaniment may develop quite naturally. In a simple
keyboard arrangement (example **4a**), the right hand could play the
melody, while the left hand part is built upon the notes of your chosen
chords. Notes other than the root, 3rd and 5th of the chord can also be
added if you wish, as shown in example **4b**:

(a)

(b)

5 Decide how to arrange your accompaniment.

The piano or keyboard part does not have to include the melody, but if
it does not, it must have its own staves, as shown in **5a**. The parts
should be aligned correctly (see Chapter 18, *Presentation*). The
accompaniment could also include a counter-melody as in example **5b**.
Some performance details have also been added.

(a)

6 Transposition.

If your solo instrument is a transposing instrument (see *Rudiments and Reference* section), the music for either the solo instrument or keyboard instrument must be transposed into the correct key. The melody below has been transposed for B♭ trumpet.

ASSIGNMENTS

1 Find copies of the following music and, for each one, compare the accompaniment with the melody. State whether both are similar or whether there is some independence in each part.

   a a pop song with the vocal part written on a separate stave and the piano or keyboard part written on two staves below.

   b a song other than a pop song, written with a piano or keyboard accompaniment.

   c a composition for a solo instrument with piano or keyboard accompaniment.

2 Compose either **(a)** a piece of music for solo instrument with piano or keyboard accompaniment, or **(b)** a song (your own choice of words) with piano or keyboard accompaniment. Write out the composition with the melody on the top stave and the piano or keyboard part beneath on two additional staves. Add a title, tempo, dynamics and any other appropriate performance details. Record your music, either performing it with a friend, or performing both parts yourself with the aid of multi-track recording equipment or computer-linked equipment.

Introductions

Many different types of compositions feature an introduction which is played before the melody, song, or main part of the music begins. The introduction sets the opening mood, and can take many forms. In many cases, it is based on ideas which occur later in the composition. Composers often use the last bars of the melody or composition, or a musical phrase, or a theme from the composition, in the introduction. Occasionally, the introduction consists of a few bars of the accompaniment but without the melody or theme. Some pop songs begin with just a rhythm (such as a drum beat), a chord sequence, unaccompanied singing, or a riff, but this is usually based upon material which is found in the song (see Chapter 10, *Composing a pop song*).

ASSIGNMENT

Choose three pieces of music each of which has an introduction (songs with piano accompaniment may be very suitable). Find out where the musical ideas featured in the introduction appear in each song. Write brief notes about your findings.

SUMMARY ASSIGNMENT

Figure 7.2 is a composition featuring many of the aspects that have been illustrated in Chapters 1–7. The music, *Last of the summer wine*, is arranged for piano or a keyboard instrument.

Study and, if possible, perform this composition. Write about the melody, accompaniment, chords and the introduction. You may also wish to comment on the use of repetition, and any other points of interest in the music.

Figure 7.2   *Last of the summer wine*   Ronnie Hazlehurst

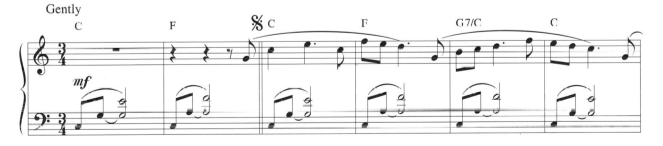

8
Words and music

Words can provide a strong stimulus for your compositions, either as a text for a song, or as a piece to be spoken with a musical accompaniment. They can also generate ideas for a composition, even if the words are not used in the final product.

Poetry

Poetry provides an endless source of inspiration to the composer, reflecting all manner of moods, situations and experiences. The poems in Figure 8.1 could be used in a variety of ways. The words of the poems could be set to music as songs, or music could be created to accompany a reading of each poem. Having chosen a poem, you may simply wish to compose some music upon the same theme, perhaps using only the title of the poem for your composition.

Figure 8.1

Two poems   Edward Lear

There was an old man with a beard,
Who said, 'It is just as I feared!-
Two Owls and a Hen,
Four Larks and a Wren,
Have all built their nests in my beard!'

There was a Young Lady of Ryde,
Whose shoe-strings were seldom untied;
She purchased some clogs
And some small spotty dogs,
And frequently walked about Ryde.

From a Railway Carriage   Robert Louis Stevenson

Faster than fairies, faster than witches,
Bridges and houses, hedges and ditches;
And charging along, like troops in a battle,
All through the meadows the horses and cattle:
All of the sights of the hill and the plain
Fly as thick as driving rain;
And ever again, in the wink of an eye,
Painted stations whistle by.

Here is a child who clambers and scrambles,
All by himself and gathering brambles;
Here is a tramp who stands and gazes;
And there is a green for stringing the daisies!
Here is a cart run away in the road
Lumping along with man and load;
And here is a mill and there is a river:
Each a glimpse and gone for ever!

Winter   Gareth Owen

On Winter mornings in the playground
The boys stand huddled,
Their cold hands doubled
Into trouser pockets.
The air hangs frozen
About the buildings
And the cold is an ache in the blood
And a pain on the tender skin
Beneath finger nails.
The odd shouts
Sound off like struck iron
And the sun
Balances white
Above the boundary wall.
I fumble my bus ticket
Between numb fingers
Into a fag,
Take a drag
And blow white smoke
Into the December air.

Lullaby   Adrian Henri

Woken and then lulled by the seagulls
Sleep till the sea-fret rolls by
Turn on your pillow till morning
Back to the opening sky

Sleep though the dreams may come crowding
like mists across the bay
Night-birds will hover above you
Cry to the echoing day

Sleep tho' the aeroplanes lull you
Dull through the evening skies
Sleep with the seabirds for guardians
Distances lost in their eyes

Sandpipers wade in the marshes
Curlews awake on the plain
Turn to the cobblestone sunlight
Wake to morning again.

Jabberwocky   Lewis Carroll

'Twas brillig, and the slithy toves
Did gyre and gimble in the wabe;
All mimsy were the borogoves
And the mome raths outgrabe.

'Beware the Jabberwock, my son!
The jaws that bite, the claws that catch!
Beware the Jubjub bird, and shun
The frumious Bandersnatch!'

He took his vorpal sword in hand:
Long time the manxome foe he sought—
So rested he by the Tumtum tree,
And stood awhile in thought.

And as in uffish thought he stood,
The Jabberwock, with eyes of flame,
Came whiffling through the tulgey wood,
And burbled as it came!

One, two! One, two! And through and through
The vorpal blade went snicker-snack!
He left it dead, and with its head
He went galumphing back.

'And hast thou slain the Jabberwock?
Come to my arms, my beamish boy!
O frabjous day! Callooh! Callay!'
He chortled in his joy.

'Twas brillig, and the slithy toves
Did gyre and gimble in the wabe;
All mimsy were the borogoves,
And the mome raths outgrabe.

Lochinvar   Sir Walter Scott

O, young Lochinvar is come out of the West!
Through all the wide border his steed was the best;
And save his good broadsword he weapons had none;
He rode all unarmed and he rode all alone.
So faithful in love and so dauntless in war,
There never was knight like the young Lochinvar!

(This is the first verse only of this poem)

ASSIGNMENTS

1 Choose one of the given poems and either set the words to music as a song, or use the poem as a starting point for a composition.

2 Using a poem of your own choice, set the words to music as a song, or compose music to accompany a reading of the poem.

3 Listen to the setting of *From a Railway Carrlage*, part of Malcolm Williamson's *From a Child's Garden*.

Found poems

Found poems can be very useful to the composer, often producing unexpected and interesting results. The technique is quite simple. To create a found poem, you need an old newspaper or magazine and a pair of scissors. You may also require some glue, although this is not essential. Cut out any words from the newspaper or magazine (perhaps about 30 or 40) and arrange them in random order. Some of the words may make a sentence or phrase which could be the starting point for a composition. With further rearrangement of the words, you may even be able to produce a poem. If you are not happy with the result, jumble up the words and start again, or add some new words.

Once you have decided upon the final arrangement of the cut-out words, you can either glue the individual words in the required order on to a sheet of paper, or just write down the words for future use. Don't expect to produce a complete poem every time using this method. Sometimes the results are disappointing, but occasionally this method will produce startling combinations of words. Figure 8.2 is an example of a Found Poem.

Figure 8.2

ASSIGNMENT

Create a Found Poem and use it as a starting point for a composition.

Prose

Prose, too, can be a powerful source of ideas. Read the two extracts in Figure 8.3 and consider the musical ideas that could develop from them.

Figure 8.3

Extract 1: A description of Coketown from *Hard Times* by Charles Dickens

It was a town of machinery and tall chimneys, out of which interminable serpents of smoke trailed themselves for ever and ever, and never got uncoiled.

It had a black canal in it, and a river that ran purple with ill-smelling dye, and vast piles of building full of windows where there was a rattling and a trembling all day long, and where the piston of the steam-engine worked monotonously up and down, like the head of an elephant in a state of melancholy madness. It contained several large streets all very like one another, and many small streets still more like one another, inhabited by people equally like one another, who went in and out at the same hours, with the same sound upon the same pavements, to do the same work, and to whom every day was the same as yesterday and tomorrow, and every year the counterpart of the last and next . . .

Extract 2: from *Cider with Rosie* by Laurie Lee

We could hear the pond as we ran down the hill, the shouts that only water produces, the squeal of skates, the ring of the ice and its hollow heaving grumble. Then we saw it; black and flat as a tray, the skaters rolling round it like marbles. We broke into a shout and charged upon it and fell sprawling in all directions. This magic substance, with its deceptive gifts, was something I could never master. It put wings on my heels and gave me the motions of Mercury, then threw me down on my nose. Yet it chose its own darlings, never the ones you supposed, the dromedary louts of the schoolroom, who came skating past with one leg in the air, who twirled and simpered, and darted like swifts; and never fell once – not they.

I was one of the pedestrians, and we worked up a slide across the polished darkness. So smooth that to step on it was to glide away, while the valley slid past like oil. You could also lie prone and try to swim on the ice, kicking your arms and legs. And you saw deep down, while in that position, little bubbles like cold green stars, jagged ominous cracks, dead ribbons of lilies, drowned bulrushes loaded like rockets.

ASSIGNMENTS

I Use one of the extracts in Figure 8.3 from *Hard Times* or *Cider with Rosie* as the starting point for a composition. You could compose some music for a soloist, or group of performers, which suggests the mood of one of the extracts. Alternatively, create a piece where the words are read to your music, or set some of the words to music as a song.

Record your composition and either write out your music, or provide an annotation to explain what you have done in your music.

2 Use the extract in Figure 8.4 from *Under Milk Wood* by Dylan Thomas as the starting point for a composition. Record your composition and either write out your music, or provide an annotation to explain what you have done in your composition.

Figure 8.4

> The sunny slow lulling afternoon yawns and moons through the dozy town. The sea lolls, laps and idles in, with fishes sleeping in its lap. The meadows still as Sunday, the shut-eye tasselled bulls, the goat-and-daisy dingles, nap happy and lazy. The dumb duck-ponds snooze. Clouds sag and pillow on Llareggub Hill.

3 Find some prose to use as the starting point for a composition. Record and write out your completed composition.

In your own words

You may decide to write your own words, as prose or poetry, and base a composition upon them. Descriptions of places, people, animals, incidents, moods and feelings are some of the aspects that you could choose to write about. You could write your own words for a song, to express a personal view or interpretation of a situation. The choice and arrangement of your song-words will depend, to a large extent, upon the type of song or music you are composing. You should consider the suitability of all the words, even if it is a very simple statement that you are making.

SUMMARY ASSIGNMENT

Compose a piece of music using your own poem, prose or words as a basis. Record and write down your completed composition.

9
The blues

Bessie Smith

Despite the abolition of slavery in the USA in 1865, many black Americans continued to face great hardship and difficulty. This was reflected in the music of the times, particularly in **spirituals** (religious songs) and the blues. The blues were secular songs (non-religious), sometimes described as **sorrow-songs**. The words were simple and repeated, telling of the lives of the people who sang them, often relating their daily struggles and problems. The titles of many blues reflect their misfortune and suffering, expressed in songs such as *Depression Blues, Poor Man Blues, Prison Bound, Bad Luck Blues, Chain Gang Blues* and *Worried Man Blues*. The words to *Good Morning Blues* are shown in Figure 9.1. The blues became an important part of American musical culture as they developed from the last quarter of the nineteenth century to the present day.

Figure 9.1

Good Morning Blues   words and music by Huddie Ledbetter

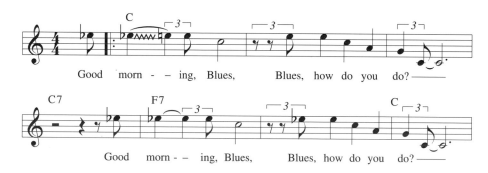

1 Good morning, Blues, Blues how do you do?
   Good morning, Blues, Blues how do you do?
   I'm do-in' all right, good morning, how are you?

2 I lay down last night, turning from side to side,
   Yes, I was turning from side to side.
   I was not sick, I was just dissatisfied.

The blues usually has a three-line stanza, with the second line repeating the first. These songs were seldom written down and were generally improvised (made up as they went along), often within a 12-bar framework. They were sung either without instrumental accompaniment or with just a guitar to support the melody. Many blues are in $\frac{4}{4}$ time. During the 1920s recordings of blues became popular, providing an exciting medium for singers, and for instrumentalists. Among the well-known blues performers were Ma Rainey, Ida Cox, Bessie Smith, Blind Lemon Jefferson, Leadbelly (Huddie Ledbetter), Lonnie Johnson and Big Bill Broonzy. Written blues, with elements of the blues structure and harmonies, appeared in the early part of the twentieth century. W C Handy's *St Louis Blues* is a well-known example.

Huddie Ledbetter (Leadbelly)

The blues scale

The blues uses its own particular scale. Built upon the degrees of a major scale (see Rudiments and Reference), the 3rd and 7th note often appears both natural and 'flattened' (lowered by one semitone). Occasionally, the 5th note is also 'flattened'. The 'flattened' notes are referred to as blue notes. Here is one way of writing a blues scale:

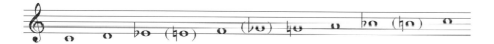

Blues Scale in the key of C

The twelve-bar blues chord sequence

Improvisation is an essential part of the blues. The pattern of chords called the 12-bar blues provides a framework for this improvisation. The 12-bar blues essentially uses three chords: those built on the tonic (I), subdominant (IV) and dominant (V) notes of the scale. In the key of C major, the pattern looks like this:

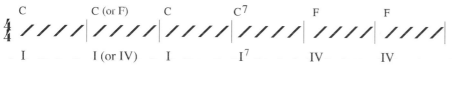

The 12-bar blues chord sequence

Repeat as necessary

Syncopation

A common feature of blues and jazz is the free use of syncopation. The effect is achieved by placing an accent on a normally weak beat, or by using a tie to prolong a note over a strong beat. Syncopation may also be produced by using a rest on a normally strong beat. In blues and jazz, however, syncopation is usually the result of improvised, natural singing and playing and is often easier to perform than to write down.

In syncopation, the normal rhythm accent is displaced onto a beat which is not usually accented.

ASSIGNMENTS

1 Listen to some recordings of the blues, noting carefully the chord sequence and structure of the music. Write brief notes about the music, commenting upon the mood, presentation, use of words (if it is a vocal blues), repetition and improvisation.

2 Use the 12-bar blues in C as the basis for an improvisation. You could work with a friend, with one person playing the chords on a keyboard instrument or a guitar, while the other person improvises an instrumental or vocal part. Alternatively, you could try to play the chords (with your left hand) and also improvise a melodic line (with your right hand) on a keyboard instrument. Record your improvisation.

3 Figure 9.2 is a blues that could be played by a number of instruments improvising around the basic chords suggested. Perform the music with some friends and record the results. If the melody is played by a transposing instrument, then transpose either the chords or the melody, as appropriate.

Figure 9.2

Montana Blues   C Binns

Bass figuration

Developing within the framework of the blues, the figurations or patterns for keyboard left hand or bass in Figure 9.3, have evolved. These may provide a useful starting point for a blues, rock or pop composition. The complete blues sequence has not been written out, as the patterns repeat each time one of the three chords is used. The examples are written in the key of C major.

ASSIGNMENT

Use one of the patterns of Figure 9.3 as the basis for an improvisation or blues composition.

Figure 9.3 Some bass figurations

The influence of the blues upon twentieth-century music, particularly jazz and pop, has been considerable. There are countless examples of pop music which feature the 12-bar blues chord sequence and the blues scale. Blues also covers a wide range of styles and attitudes in music, from the early unaccompanied songs first heard over one hundred years ago, through to sophisticated, blues-influenced instrumental and vocal music performed today .

Figure 9.4 is an example of a blues-influenced composition. The music does not use the basic three-chord structure but, like all blues and much blues-influenced music, it has a particular blues 'feel' to it. This composition can be performed either by solo piano or by a small group with a solo instrument such as trumpet or saxophone, accompanied by piano or keyboard, bass and drums. The mood is relaxed and improvisation around the chord sequence and melody is encouraged.

Figure 9.4   · *Melody in Blue*   C Binns

SUMMARY ASSIGNMENT

Compose a vocal or instrumental piece of music with a blues 'feel' which includes elements of improvisation. The composition may be for a solo performer or for a group of perrformers. You may wish to write down a chord sequence or a melody as a starting point. Give your composition a title and record the music. As improvisation is a very important element of the blues, each performance of your composition could be quite different.

10

Composing a pop song

Pop music is one aspect of the music world which is constantly reacting to new and exciting developments. There are many different styles of pop music and each presents opportunities for you to explore. Composing a pop song is quite a challenge and needs a lot of practice, but it can be great fun. However, like many aspects of composition, explaining how to do it is rather difficult. The theory and basic principles can be taught, but effective compositions will only be achieved after much practice, experimentation and critical listening. Listen to a wide range of successful groups and singers and try to identify those elements which make their songs so effective. In your own work, start by copying styles and presentations of successful pop musicians. It is the method by which most of us learn.

Before you begin to compose a pop song, think about the ultimate performance and the resources available. It is no use creating an exciting phrase or riff especially for saxophone if no one can actually play that instrument, nor re-create that sound on a synthesiser or electronic keyboard instrument. Neither is it of much use to write a piece which is too difficult to perform. Try to compose for the resources at hand, otherwise you may never actually hear your music as you intended. You may know a pop group who would try out your ideas, or be in a group yourself.

You could also use a multi-track recording machine and play some, or all, of the instruments yourself. Electronic keyboards are very useful for this purpose, providing a wide variety of sounds, including drum-kit rhythms. You could add your own vocals using the multi-track recorder, or ask a friend to help if you do not want to sing yourself.

Whatever you compose, ensure that it is playable, and that you have the resources to realise your composition.

Words or music first?

There are two ways to compose your pop song. Start with the words and let the composition grow around them, or start with the music and add the words later. Both these methods can be explored by experimenting with your instrument, trying out different combinations of words and music, or letting your pop group pick up some of the ideas and play around with them until something suitable develops.

Starting with the words

Some people find it easier to compose a song if they have the words to begin with. The first problem to overcome is where to find the words. Ideas are suggested in Chapter 8, *Words and music*. You may wish to use one of the suggestions to help you get started. Pop music words, however, are not always easy to find. Poems may be useful, but some verse may be inappropriate and difficult to set to music because of the irregular length of lines or choice of words. It may be easier to write your own words or find a friend who is good with words and form a song writing duo. If you are stuck for words or you are not very keen on writing poetry, try using a found poem. You can create some strange and exciting lines with this approach.

Basic guidelines for writing a pop song

1 **Keep it simple.**

Don' t make the song too long or too complicated.

2 **Plan and shape the music.**

Develop a plan (or form) for your pop song which features an introduction, verses, chorus (or refrain) and an ending. The pattern may look like this:

Introduction (music only) - verse 1 - verse 2 - chorus - verse 1 (repeat) - chorus - chorus - final chorus fade to end

This plan is only a suggestion. There are many other ways to organise a song. For example, you do not always need to start with an introduction. Many songs simply begin straight away with the chorus. Also, the plan for a longer song could include additional sections which feature different words, instrumental verses, and new musical ideas. Some songs also include a **coda**, which is a short, rounding-off section ending the song.

3 **Sort out the words.**

Once you have some words, decide which is verse and which is chorus. You could use as few as 12 lines, which may be arranged as follows:

Verse 1 (4 lines), verse 2 (4 new lines), chorus (4 new lines), verse 1 (repeat), chorus (repeat), chorus (repeat), chorus fade (repeat).

However, if you do try to get your message across in only 12 lines, avoid over-simplicity and too much repetition.

4 **Try to make the words scan.**

The number of syllables in each line should form some sort of pattern with a sense of balance.

For example: Line 1 — 7 syllables to this rhythm: ♩♩♩♩|♩♩♩|

Line 2 — 5 syllables to this rhythm: ♩♩♩♩|♩. |

Line 3 — 7 syllables as in line 1: ♩♩♩♩|♩♩♩|

Line 4 — 5 syllables as line 2: ♩♩♩♩|♩. ‖

Knowing the number of syllables in each line will help if you are writing your own words, particularly if you are having difficulties thinking of a new line.

5 Try to accent the important words or syllables.

6 Re-examine the impact of the words.

Before you add any music, read the words through again and be critical. Will they hold the listener's attention, or are they really rather dull? If they are dull, rewrite them. There should be no excuse for using mediocre, bland words (or music) that are of no interest to the listener. You should aim to communicate.

7 Experiment with the music.

Once you have found the words and taken a few basic decisions about the song, start to put some music to them. Many of the suggestions given in Chapter 5 will apply. Think about the mood, the key and the tempo of the piece, and experiment with ideas on your instrument. You may find it useful to try to sing the words as well. Perhaps the words will suggest a rhythm or a melodic phrase.

Once you have an idea, expand it, but be economical. You can often repeat or extend a good musical phrase in a song to give a feeling of unity, rather than constantly introducing new material. In Figure 10.1, for example, the shape of the opening phrase of *Sound of Silence* by Paul Simon is repeated or adapted. There is also a connection between some of the notes of each phrase of the melody and the accompanying chord.

Figure 10.1   *Sound of Silence*   Paul Simon

For example, the melody notes in bar 1 are D, F and A, and the accompanying chord is one of D minor.

Often it is the chorus or a particular riff of your song which is memorable. A good commercial pop song often has at least one aspect that is instantly memorable. Even after just one hearing the listener remembers part of the tune. This is what you should aim to achieve.

The process

Figure 10.2 describes the process of writing a song, including the first steps in putting a melody to words, and some of the ways in which various possibilities were explored. The song, *Song for Youth*, was written for International Youth Year and intended to be in the pop idiom for a mass schools' choir. The mood was lyrical and optimistic.

Figure 10.2   *Song for Youth (Composer's annotation)*

I organised most of the words of the song before I began to compose the melody. Then, I worked at the piano, experimenting with different musical ideas, thinking about the rhythm of the words and trying to find a suitable melody. The first line of the song was 'Look all around you, see what surrounds you'. and below are some of my early thoughts about a possible melody for these words. Any one of the following examples could have been used. In fact, I worked on far more than are given below. However, in the end, I decided on theme (e) which seemed to contain a sufficient number of the elements for which I was looking. It was bright, punchy and positive. I followed the first two bars as given below, with another two bars of similar shape, and then repeated the melody of bars 1 and 2 in bars 5 and 6. Note also how bar 2 is simply a repeat of the melody in bar 1 but with a different chord accompaniment. I like the idea of letting a good theme 'earn its keep' by using it in various guises with rhythmic, melodic and harmonic developments all coming from the original germ of the main theme.

As the song began to take shape, I tried out many different harmonies (or chords) until eventually I was satisfied with the result. I made a written copy of the song for my own use which included the melody line, the chords and the words. This is how the first verse and refrain looked:

Figure 10.2 continued

Often, this type of music score is quite sufficient, particularly if you are playing the music yourself, or in a small group.

However, in this case, I knew that the song would be performed by a very large number of singers from about a dozen choirs and that several people would have to teach the song to them before they all finally came together. While the score was suitable for the singers, it did not give enough information about how the piano accompaniment should be performed. It was, therefore, also necessary to write out an accurate piano score complete with the vocal part.

Having done this, I finally set to work on an arrangement, based on the piano accompaniment, for the brass band which would accompany the choir on the first public performance of the song.

C Binns

Starting with the music

Writing the music for a pop song before you've written the words is a common way to approach composing. Your final composition will be a blend of chords (harmonies), melody (the vocal or instrumental line), rhythmic drive and instrumental colour.

Whether you begin with a melody or chords will depend upon the instruments which you play. Keyboard players and guitarists will often work on a chord pattern or sequence, while other instrumentalists and singers may compose the melody first and fix the chords later. It does not really matter which way round you choose to work. Choose the way that is the most comfortable for you.

Once you have some ideas about the melody or chord structure, continue to work at it until it is exactly what you want. Figure 10.3 contains some of the questions which you could consider when composing your pop song. Working from a chord-based approach, the given musical idea prompts a variety of possibilities to be tried out.

Riffs

> **Like an ostinato, a riff is a repeated, usually short, musical pattern such as a rhythmic or melodic phrase. Chords may also be added to a melodic riff.**

A riff is a very useful device which is often used in jazz and pop music. It is usually played by the group or band, while one of the instruments improvises against this repetitive theme. It can also serve as a link, as an introduction or as the main theme of the composition. A simple riff can develop into longer, impressive phrases or even spark off a whole composition. Sometimes the entire group plays the same melodic riff in unison with no harmonies. The effect can be very dramatic. Alternatively, in some pop music, a short chord sequence is repeated many times by the group, while one performer, such as the lead guitarist, saxophonist or keyboard player, improvises. For example, a simple chord sequence such as:

could be repeated many times by rhythm guitar, bass guitar, and keyboard with drums while the lead guitar adds an improvised part. Figure 10.4 shows a four-bar riff from the Chris de Burgh song *What about me?* The riff consists of a short melodic theme supported by chords and adds great impact to the song.

Instrumentation What instrument will play this? A piano or electronic keyboard? Or perhaps a combination of instruments such as keyboard with trumpet, saxophone, guitar, bass guitar and drums? How will I allocate parts to the group? Who will play what?

Key Am I in the correct key? [If someone is going to sing in this key, remember their vocal range.] If I like working in this key and discover it should be higher or lower when I've finished, I'll have to transpose it. If I intend to add brass I must be careful to avoid keys with a lot of sharps.

Form Is this the introduction, the verse or the chorus?

Tempo At what speed shall I play this? [Try a few different speeds until you are satisfied.] Should I speed up or slow down in the music?

Chords What chord next? E minor then C major, or what about B minor then C major? Are there other chords that would fit? Or should I repeat these chords and the phrase again before introducing new chords? At the moment I've a pedal bass on G (this means the G stays even though the chord moves to A minor). Should I continue this pedal bass over the next few bars? If so, when do I change the pedal note?

Dynamics Will it be loud all the way through, or will there be contrasting sections where it is quieter?

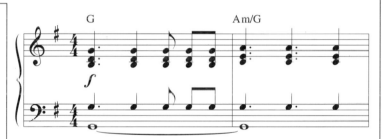

Words Shall I add some words to this phrase?

Rhythm This looks like a complicated rhythm. Should I have a simpler one? Will I use this rhythm as the basis for my song or should I develop it further? Do I really intend the rhythm to sound like this? Do I perhaps mean:

or

Originality Does it sound like someone else's song? [If so, be careful! I am trying to write an original work here.]

Melody At some point I want to add a melody line. Should it have the same rhythm as the opening phrase, like this:

Or would a smoother, contrasting melody with longer notes be better? Something like this:

or this

Finally Have I explored all the possibilities from this opening? Am I satisfied with the final outcome?

Figure 10.3 Points to consider when composing a pop song

Figure 10.4
What about me?
Chris de Burgh

ASSIGNMENTS

1 Listen to the Chris De Burgh song *What about me?* from the album *Into the Light*. Identify where the riff shown in Figure 10.4 occurs.

2 Find three examples of pop songs which feature a riff. Listen for a short repeated chord sequence, for example, with perhaps a guitar improvising above this pattern. Write brief notes about each example, naming the instruments which play the riff, and identifying the instruments or voices which perform a 'solo' at the same time. If possible, count how many times the riff is repeated in the song.

3 Figure 10.5 provides some repeating chord sequences for you to play and experiment with. Choose an appropriate tempo for each, and try out the sequences either on your own, or with others. You may adapt the given ideas if you wish. For example, you could add extra bars, repeat chords, or transpose the sequence to a different key.

    a Add an improvised melody to each of the repeating chord sequences in Figure 10.5.

Figure 10.5 Repeating chord sequences

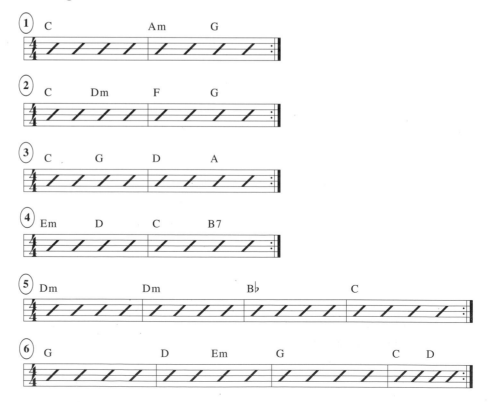

b Figure 10.6 shows some short melodic riffs with suggested chords. Try to improvise a melody while the riff is repeated as many times as necessary. The riff could be played by a friend, or a group of friends, or recorded on tape.

Figure 10.6 Melodic riffs with chords

Chris de Burgh

c Use one of the riffs in Figure 10.6 as a starting point for your own pop song or instrumental composition.

4 Compose a riff and use it in your own composition.

Instrumental breaks

Many pop songs feature an instrumental break or solo. Often, the soloist plays an instrumental version of the verse or chorus, or improvises while the rest of the group repeat the music for the verse or the chorus. There are many excellent examples of instrumental breaks occurring in live or recorded pop music, although often these are not always fully written out in copies of music which you may buy. However, Figure 10.7 is an example of a very effective instrumental break which has been written out. It is from the song *Telegraph Road* by Mark Knopfler, featured on the Dire Straits album *Money For Nothing*. The first eight bars are performed by solo piano, then the other instruments in the group join in, while the lead guitar plays the melody. The first 16 bars of the break are shown.

Mark Knopfler from Dire Straits

ASSIGNMENTS

1 Listen to *Telegraph Road* from the Dire Straits album *Money For Nothing*, and in particular the instrumental break, part of which is shown in Figure 10.7.

2 Find a pop song which has an instrumental break. Describe as carefully as you can what happens in this section of the music, and how it contributes to the overall effect of the song.

Figure 10.7

Telegraph Road

words and music by Mark Knopfler

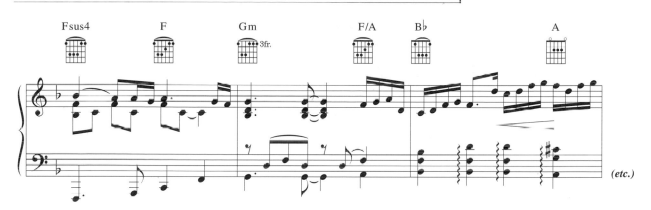

Introduction

Many pop songs begin with an introduction. This could be a few chords, a drum kit rhythm, a bass guitar riff, part or all of the verse or chorus, or some unaccompanied singing. Often, the ideas found in the introduction are taken from the verse or chorus of the song. Sometimes the introduction is different from the rest of the song, deliberately providing a contrast. Try to listen to a wide variety of pop music, including rock, reggae and soul music, taking particular note of the introduction.

While you do not always need to include an introduction in your own pop song, remember that the opening bars are important. They can set the mood, and should hold the listener's attention.

Figure 10.8

ASSIGNMENTS

1 Listen to *Bohemian Rhapsody* by Queen. Note how important the opening bars of the music are, and how the mood of the song is established. Find two aspects of these opening bars which are rather unusual features of pop music.

2 Choose two pop songs which have an introduction. For each song describe the instruments or voices which perform in the introduction. Say where the musical ideas used in the introduction occur later in the music.

How to present your music

If your pop song is to be performed by others, you will probably need to write down your ideas. This can be done in several ways. For example, you could write out the chord sequence for the group members and give the words to the singer, but you will have to explain exactly what the music requires. An alternative would be to write out the melody with words and chords added, indicating the tempo and any dynamics that you require. Often this provides sufficient information for the group. Figure 10.9 provides an example of some instrumental music written in this way for a rock group.

Figure 10.9   *Overture: The Pirate Show*   C Binns

Printed music of pop songs is usually written on two staves, as piano or keyboard music, or on three staves, with one stave for the melody, and two for the keyboard instrument. Chords are often added, sometimes with chord windows showing how to play the chord on a guitar as illustrated in Figure 10.7, *Telegraph Road*.

SUMMARY ASSIGNMENT

Use some of the ideas in this chapter as a starting point for your own pop song. You may work on your own, or as part of a group. Try to produce a score of your song with melody, chords and words, or an annotation to explain what you have done. Record the finished composition.

11
Choosing a title

One of the most difficult tasks which a composer may have to deal with is the apparently simple job of finding a suitable title for a composition. Although it is not always necessary to give your composition a title, most composers do. Sometimes, you may be inspired by a particular event, picture, poem or person, and the title of the music, which may be descriptive, humorous or instructive, will be quite obvious. A line or phrase from a song may often become the title. At other times you may think of a tune before a title even suggests itself. On such occasions finding just the right title can be extremely difficult.

Many compositions have been given memorable and appropriate titles. They include: *The Sea* (Debussy), *Billy the Kid* (Copland), *The Carnival of Animals* (Saint-Saëns), *The Sorcerer's Apprentice* (Dukas), *Rhapsody in Blue* (Gershwin), *The Firebird* (Stravinsky), *The Planets Suite* (Holst), *Enigma Variations* (Elgar), *Peter and the Wolf* (Prokofiev) and *The Flying Dutchman* (Wagner).

Many composers and editors have used a simple numbering system such as Symphony no. 4 , Fugue 16 or Opus 27. If a collection of pieces are written in the same style you could have Opus 1 no. 1, Opus 1 no. 2 and Opus 1 no. 3. Often you will see a title such as *Suite no. 1*, *Sonata for violin*, *Allegro for flute*, or *Polonaise in A*. Here, the form, style, speed or characteristics of the music dictate the title. A short glossary of useful terms which may help you to choose a title is listed below.

Adagio: (e.g. Adagio for Viola) A piece or movement in slow tempo.
Allegro: (e.g. Allegro for Flute) A piece or movement in quick tempo.
Allemande: Dance movement, often the first movement of the suite of the baroque era. In moderate $\frac{4}{4}$ time, usually beginning on a short anacrusis.
Bagatelle: Short, light piece, often for piano.
Bourrée: Dance in quick duple time, beginning with an anacrusis; sometimes found in the baroque suite.
Carol: A seasonal sacred song, most often celebrating Christmas or Easter.
Courante: A dance, often found in the baroque suite. The two types of courante are Italian and French.

George Gershwin (1898–1937)

Opus generally refers to music in a published, catalogued, or written order, so that Opus 1 comes before Opus 2.

Edward Elgar (1857–1934)

The Italian **corrente** is in $\frac{3}{4}$ or $\frac{3}{8}$ time with a lively character. The French **courante** is in $\frac{3}{2}$ or $\frac{6}{4}$, often with these two metres interchanged and the position of the accent varied.

Duet: A composition for two voices or instruments, with or without accompaniment or for two players on one keyboard.

Gavotte: A dance in $\frac{4}{4}$ time beginning on the third beat of the bar, sometimes found in the baroque suite.

Gigue or **Jig**: A fast, lively dance, usually in compound time (e.g. $\frac{6}{8}$ or $\frac{12}{8}$) and often the final movement of a suite.

Hornpipe: Originally a lively English dance in triple time ($\frac{3}{2}$ or $\frac{3}{4}$), later in $\frac{2}{4}$ or $\frac{4}{4}$.

Intermezzo: A short orchestral or piano piece. The term also refers to a short interlude between the acts of an opera.

March: A marching or processional piece in $\frac{2}{2}$, $\frac{4}{4}$ or $\frac{6}{8}$ time.

Mazurka: A Polish dance in triple time ($\frac{3}{4}$) with the second or third beat accented.

Minuet: A graceful court dance in triple time ($\frac{3}{4}$), sometimes found in the baroque suite. In the work of Haydn, Mozart and Beethoven the character of the minuet changed and the tempo became faster.

Nocturne: 'Night piece'; a short, instrumental composition, generally of a melancholy character with an expressive melody. Usually for the piano.

Passacaglia: Originally a seventeenth and eighteenth-century dance in slow triple time, the passacaglia consisted of variations built upon an ostinato or ground bass.

Polka: A lively dance in duple time ($\frac{2}{4}$) originating in Bohemia.

Polonaise: Stately Polish processional music or dance in moderate triple time ($\frac{3}{4}$).

Prélude: An instrumental introductory movement (as in the suite) or piece preceding another piece of music, such as a fugue. It can also be a short self-contained piece, often for piano.

Quartet: A composition for four voices or instruments.

Rondo: Composition in which the main tune reappears at least three times, separated by contrasting episodes. The plan of a simple rondo is A B A C A.

Sarabande: A slow, stately dance in triple time ($\frac{3}{4}$ or $\frac{3}{2}$) with an accent on the second beat. It is found in the baroque suite.

Scherzo: A fast, lively movement, found in symphonies and sonatas. The scherzo, usually in $\frac{3}{4}$ time, developed from the minuet. The term also refers to an independent instrumental piece, often for piano.

Sonata: From the Classical period onwards, the sonata, which had three or four movements, was a composition for one or two instruments. The normal plan of the movements was: **1** Fast (in Sonata Form), **2** Slow, **3** Minuet (or Scherzo) and Trio, **4** Fast.

Study (or Etude): A short instrumental piece to improve or demonstrate a particular aspect of technique.

Suite: The baroque suite consisted of a set of instrumental dance movements, generally all in the same key. The dances were the allemande, courante, sarabande and gigue. Various other types of dances (such as the gavotte or bourrée) were sometimes added, and an introductory movement, such as a prélude, could also be found. The term is also applied to more recent instrumental compositions, consisting of several related movements.

Trio: A composition for three voices or instruments. In the minuet or scherzo movement of a sonata (or symphony, etc.), the term is also used to indicate a second, contrasting minuet (or scherzo), preceding the return of the first.

Variations (or **Theme and variations**): A musical theme is stated then repeated many times with modifications and elaborations to the melody, rhythm and harmony.

Waltz: A dance in triple time ($\frac{3}{4}$), frequently harmonised with only one chord to each bar.

SUMMARY ASSIGNMENTS

1 Choose one of the above terms as a title and starting point for a composition.

2 Find six examples of compositions, each with a title which includes one of the above terms. Note the instruments for which the piece was written and the composer. For example, *Polonaise in A♭ major*, for piano, by Chopin.

3 Compose a collection (or suite) of pieces, each with its own character and title, but linked by a common theme using one of the following suggestions:

Days of the week; Animals; Weather; Insects; Seasons; School; Friends; Colours; Moods; Machines; Birds; The Fair.

4 Compose a group of pieces based upon a title of your own choice.

5 Find a collection of pieces which are linked by a common theme. Note the composer and the instruments for which the music was written. List the name of each piece or movement.

6 Some titles which you could use for your compositions are listed in Figure 11.1. Choose one of the titles as a starting point for a composition.

Figure 11.1

Train Ride	The Clock Shop	Clouds	From a Window
Goblins Gathering	The Magic Carpet	Reflections	The Machine
Sleepwalking	Mr Wilson's Cat	The City Sleeps	Conversations
Morning Mists	Footsteps	The Desert	The River
Festive March	February	Quiet Moments	Volcano
The Stream	Daydreams	Seahorse	In the Hills
The Waterwheel	Slow Waltz	A Canal Journey	Spring
The Hunt	The Dream	Light and Shade	Camels
The Old Witch	The Surprise	Messages	A Woodland Scene
Visions	The Clown	A Country Walk	Seaspray
Storm at Sea	Folkdance	Dashing Mr. Bellamy	Hocus-Pocus
A Sad Melody	The Dark Cave	The Return	The Wolf
Creepy Crawlies	Sunrise	Aliens	Horace the Spider
Sandstorm	Dino's Theme	Joyful Jig	The Mysterious
Underwater	The Eagle	Music for a	Mountain
Adventure	Octopus	Celebration	

12
Form in music

Form in music is the plan or structure upon which the music is built. Form gives the music a sense of balance and shape, enabling the composer to organise it, while helping the listener to understand the composer's intentions. There are many types of form; some very simple, others more complicated and its use occurs in nearly all the music which we hear, whether it is classical, modern, jazz or pop. We have seen in Chapter 3 some of the different ways in which composers use elements of repetition and how this device can be used to extend, develop or provide the framework of a composition. The structure of many musical forms is created by the repetition of sections of a piece of music, often with other contrasting sections interspersed. This chapter gives information on the four forms which are commonly found, these being **binary** form, **ternary** form, **rondo** form and **variation** form. It also gives guidelines on how to use form in your own compositions.

Binary form

Binary form is one of the oldest and simplest forms. It was widely used from 1650 to 1750, particularly in dance movements by Bach, Couperin, Handel, Purcell and Scarlatti. Binary form has two sections, A and B, and there are many simple melodies (such as Figure 12.1) which have this structure. The two sections are often presented with repeats, AABB, and the music is usually written with repeat signs like this: ‖: A :‖: B :‖.

Figure 12.1   *Weggis*   Traditional

Figure 12.2   *Rigadoon*   H Purcell

Figure 12.2 is a rigadoon by the composer Henry Purcell. The music is in binary form and each section is repeated.

To provide an element of contrast in binary form, a modulation (or change of key) is often found, with each section organised as follows:

- section A begins in the tonic key (or main key of the whole piece) and modulates to the dominant;

- section B begins in the new key (dominant) and works back (sometimes through a number of other keys) to the original key (tonic).

A rigadoon (or rigaudon) was a lively seventeenth-century dance.

In the following march in Figure 12.3, the first section (A) begins in the key of D major and ends in the key of A major, while the second section (B) begins in the key of A major, returning to D major by the end of the piece. The melody only of this keyboard piece is shown.

Figure 12.3   *March* from the *Anna Magdalena Notebook*   C P E Bach

Allegro

ASSIGNMENTS

1 Compose a melody in binary form. You may add chords, harmonisation or an accompaniment to your melody if you wish.

2 Find a composition that is in binary form. State the title of the music and the name of the composer (if known). Say how long section A and section B are, and name the key of the music, or the keys through which it passes. If possible, perform the music or listen to a recording of it.

Ternary form

Ternary form has three sections, the third section being a repeat of the first. It can be represented as A B A, as A A B A or as A : ‖ : B A : ‖ . Figure 12.4 is a melody in ternary form. Figure 12.5 is a longer piece of music in ternary form. Section A , with its repeat, is followed by section B, and finishes with a restatement of section A. The melody is written for violin; the piano accompaniment has been omitted.

Figure 12.4   *The Bluebells of Scotland*   Scottish traditional

Figure 12.5   *In the Greenwood*   C Binns

Ternary form is still used by composers today, while early examples can be found in the minuets of Mozart and Haydn. If the third section is an exact repeat of the first section, as in Figure 12.5, composers often write Da Capo or D.C. ('from the beginning') at the end of the middle section. The sections need not be of great length, but there may be subdivisions or repeated passages in each section. The key of each section in ternary form is usually:

Section A - Tonic key

Section B - New key, often closely related to the tonic key such as the dominant or relative minor (or relative major)

Section A - Tonic key

The first and last sections (A) are usually the same or very similar, while the middle section (B) often provides a contrast.

Short pieces in binary and ternary form were sometimes combined to produce one larger movement in ternary form. For example, the Minuet and Trio of the classical period was, in fact, two minuets, the second of which, if an orchestral or instrumental ensemble composition, was often performed by only three instruments. Each minuet would be structured in binary or ternary form and the plan of the whole movement would look like this:

Minuet I	Trio (Minuet II)	Minuet I (repeat)
A1 :‖: B A2 :	C1 :‖: D C2 :‖	A1 ‖ B A2 ‖

- The form of the Trio here, could also be designated A1 - B - A2, but has been identified as C1 - D - C2 to indicate that the musical themes are different from those of Minuet I.

- On the return of Minuet I (following the trio), repeats are usually omitted.

Each minuet is written in ternary form. However, as the overall plan of the music also has three sections (or minuets), with the third being a repeat of the first, the piece could also be said to be in ternary form. To avoid confusion, this form is often referred to as **Minuet and Trio form**.

ASSIGNMENTS

1 Compose a melody in ternary form. You may add chords, harmonisation or an accompaniment to your melody if you wish.

2 Find a composition that is in ternary form. State the title of the music and the name of the composer. Say how many bars there are in each section, and name the key of the music, or the keys through which the music passes. If possible, perform the music or listen to a recording of it.

3 Listen to a Minuet and Trio from a symphony by Mozart or Haydn and study the relevant score. Write brief notes about the way in which the music is organised, and comment on the number of bars and key(s) of each section of the music. If you are unsure of which symphony to choose, you could select the third movement from Mozart's *Symphony No. 39 in E♭, K 543*.

Rondo form

Rondo form was frequently used for the final movement of the classical sonata, concerto and symphony, and is really an extension of ternary form. It can be illustrated as A B A C A, but can also be A B A C A D . . . A with as many contrasting sections as appropriate. The main theme recurs throughout the composition with different sections or tunes (called **episodes**) in between. The episodes often provide contrast and are also in different keys.

A movement written in rondo form can be quite lengthy. You could listen to one of the following two well-known movements by Mozart, each of which illustrates rondo form: Third movement from *Horn Concerto No.3 in E♭* or *Rondo (Alla Turca)* from *Piano Sonata in A major K.33l*.

ASSIGNMENTS

1 Compose a melody in rondo form using the plan A B A C A or A B A C A D A. You may add chords, harmonies or an accompaniment to your melody.

2 Select and develop at least three of the eight themes in Figure 12.6 to use in your own composition in rondo form, using the plan A B A C A or A B A C A D A. Theme A, which you should extend or change as necessary, is suggested as the main theme of section A . However, you may then choose any of the other themes to use in sections B and C (and D). For example, you may choose Theme 3 as the basis of your section B and Theme 7 as the basis of your section C. Whichever themes you select, each should be extended and developed into perhaps eight or 16 bars.

Your rondo may be for solo instrument, such as flute, violin or piano, or for an instrument with piano accompaniment. You may also compose for a group of instruments if you wish. Suggested harmonies (or chords) for Theme A are given, and a suitable chord is also recommended for the opening note or notes of each additional theme. You may, of course, choose any appropriate harmonies for your composition.

3 Find a composition in rondo form. You may choose either of the two pieces by Mozart suggested above if you wish. Write a brief description of the composition, commenting on the different sections which occur in the music.

Figure 12.6 Themes to use in Assignment 2

Theme A (this should become the theme of your section A).

Now select themes from the following for your section B and section C (and section D):

Theme 1   Theme 2

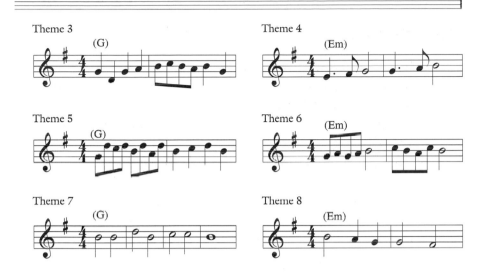

Theme 3 (G)

Theme 4 (Em)

Theme 5 (G)

Theme 6 (Em)

Theme 7 (G)

Theme 8 (Em)

Variation form

For centuries, composers have used elements of variation in their music with melodic embroidering (ornaments such as trills and turns), and rhythmic, harmonic and contrapuntal variation.

Perhaps the most important type of variation is found in the **Theme and Variations** or **Air with Variations** form. In this form, a musical idea (the theme or subject) is presented and then returns in various disguises and with many modifications (the variations). Variations can appear as a composition in their own right, for example, Bach's *Goldberg Variations*, Beethoven's *Diabelli Variations*, and Elgar's *Enigma Variations*, or they can appear as a movement of a work such as a sonata or symphony. The theme is usually a short, simple tune and may be original or borrowed from another composer, such as Britten's *Variations on a Theme of Henry Purcell*.

Harmonic variation refers to changes in the harmony or choice of chords. Contrapuntal variation refers to the ways in which the melodic lines can be woven together differently.

How to compose variations

Below are some suggestions to help you compose a theme with variations. Any, or all, of the following ideas may be used in your composition, and the number of variations you write is your decision. Some composers have written over 30 variations on one theme, but you do not need to write that many!

The theme

Choose a simple theme, perhaps eight, 12 or 16 bars in length. You may either write your own theme or borrow a tune. Nursery rhymes, for example, have often been used. Figure 12.7 shows the opening bars of a simple theme (1).

Variations

There follow some of the ways in which the theme may be varied. The theme or melody (1) can be written out at a **different pitch** (2) or in a **different key** (3). The theme can be extended by **sequence** (4) or simply be added to and **elaborated** (5). **Dynamics** and **phrasing** can also be added (4 and 5). **Ornaments** may be used to good effect (6). A **counter-melody** or **descant** may be added (7). The **rhythm** can be varied (8), or the **time signature** and the **number of beats in a bar** (9) can be changed. A **tempo** direction (10) may also be included and changed with each variation.

As well as presenting the theme in a different key, for example, moving the theme from C major to D major (3), we can **change from a major key to a minor key** (11) or vice versa. The theme is now presented, in example 11, in the key of C minor, and the mood of the music is changed. The **chords** (12 and 13), **harmony** (14) or **accompaniment** (15) can also be varied.

The **style**, **character** or **texture** of the music can be extensively changed. The music can, for example, be written as a march or a waltz, in the classical or pop style, or as a canon or even a fugue. Example 16 shows how the theme could be presented with a rather bold and dramatic character. The music, for piano, has moved to the key of C minor.

Figure 12.7

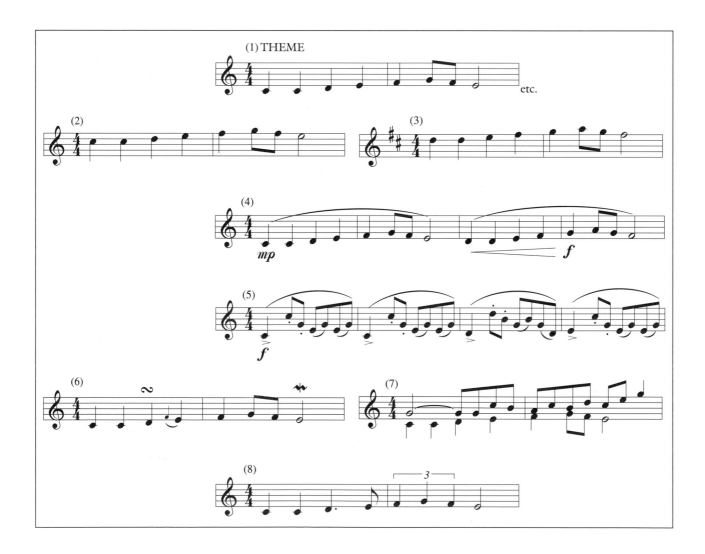

If the composition is for a group of instruments then it is also possible to **vary the instruments** which play the theme. In this way, a greater variety of musical colour and texture is added. Variations are often written for solo instrument with piano or keyboard accompaniment. In many such pieces the variations for the solo performer become more and more demanding as the music develops, while the piano accompaniment often remains fairly simple and supportive.

ASSIGNMENTS

1 Compose your own theme and a set of variations for a solo instrument, or for solo instrument with piano or keyboard accompaniment.

2 Select one of the nursery rhyme melodies in Figure 12.8 as the theme upon which to compose your own variations. Your composition may be for one instrument, a solo instrument with piano or keyboard accompaniment, or for a group of instruments.

3 Find an example of one composition written in Theme and Variation form. Listen to a recording of the music and study the score. Write brief notes about the theme and each variation.

Figure 12.8

A   *The little nut tree*

B   *Little Bo-Peep*

C   *Polly, Put the Kettle on*

How to use form

There are many ways in which binary, ternary, rondo and variation form can be adapted when you organise your music. Many folk songs use a simple binary form, structured as verse (A) and refrain (B) repeated as many times as necessary. The song may be structured like this: *verse 1 – refrain – verse 2 – refrain – verse 3 – refrain – verse 4 – refrain*, which may also be represented as A^1 B A^2 B A^3 B A^4 B. Although the words of each verse will be different in this plan, the music for each verse is the same each time. Pop songs can also be described in this way. For example, the main sections of a pop song will be the verse (A) and refrain (B) with perhaps a third section (C) containing new material. The form of some pop songs can be illustrated as:

- A1 — B — A2 — B — A3 — B — B — (B, etc.)
- A1 — A2 — B — A3 — A4 — B — B — (B, etc.).
- A1 — B — A2 — B — C — B — B — (B, etc.)
- B — A1 — B — A2 — B — B

Additional sections (D, E, F, etc.) and an introduction can be added. An ending section (called a **coda**) may also be added. This is often simply a riff from the song.

Instrumental breaks also occur frequently in pop music. However, although these often feature new, and sometimes improvised, material usually for a soloist, the break is often based upon the chord sequence of the verse or the refrain, or upon a repeated riff.

SUMMARY ASSIGNMENT

Listen to a pop song of your own choice, and use the letters A, B, C, and so on, to describe its form. Remember, it is the music, not the words, which you are describing.

13
Rounds and canons

Vocal canons, such as **rounds** and **catches**, have a long history and were particularly fashionable in England during the seventeenth and eighteenth centuries. Rounds and catches are **canons at the unison**, meaning that the second part (and any other part) is at the same pitch as the first part. In this type of canon, each voice enters in turn and, having come to the end of the melody, goes back to the beginning and repeats the melody as many times as agreed by the performers. It is also called a **perpetual canon** or **infinite canon**. It is clear where the name **round** originates from, as each voice goes 'round and round' in this type of composition. Some well-known rounds include *London's Burning, Three Blind Mice* and *Frère Jacques*. A three-part round (for three singers or three groups) with three melodic phrases (A, B, C) would look like this:

Singer 1	A	B	C	‖: A	B	C	:‖
Singer 2		A	B	‖: C	A	B	:‖
Singer 3			A	‖: B	C	A	:‖

At the end of a canon or round, each part is obviously at a different point in the melody, and only one part (in this example, singer 1) will actually be at the end of the melody.

A canon or round can be an exciting composition, whether it is for voices, or instruments. In either case, the composition techniques are the same except that a round would need some words. Two important characteristics of a round are that:

- the melody usually consists of sections or phrases of equal length.
- when performed together, the sections produce good harmony.

Composing a simple canon for three voices or instruments

Here is one method of composing an **infinite canon at the unison**:

Step 1

Organise the opening phrase of the melody. This can be of any length, but it will determine the character and remaining parts of the canon. A two-bar opening phrase could look like this:

Step 2

To carry out the second step requires a little knowledge about chords or harmony. Decide which chords will fit your melody. It does not have to be very complicated. Only two chords have been used in the illustration: a chord of C major (the notes are C, E, G), which is the tonic chord and a chord of G major (G, B, D), a chord built on the dominant.

CHORDS:

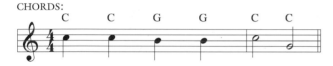

Step 3

Add the two remaining notes of each chord to every melody note, writing them underneath the melody. For the moment, each chord should only contain three notes (for example C, E, G), each note being used only once in that chord. You can either write them all on one stave (a) or on three separate staves (b).

The melody shown here works quite well, although line 2 is not very interesting. This composition needs a little more work.

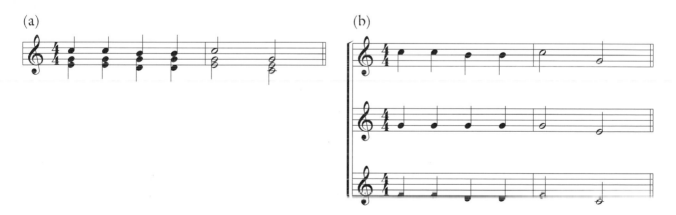

If you want to write in four parts, one note of the chord will have to appear twice. In a major key it is best to double the root or the fifth of the chord. A chord of C, for example, with the root (C) doubled, gives a chord with the notes C, E, G and C, and a chord of C with the fifth (G) doubled gives a chord with the notes C, E, G and G.

Step 4

Look at ways in which the melody can be improved. Work at the piano or with an electronic keyboard and try out different ideas. You could, for example, develop the rhythm of the melody. In this composition, the rhythm of lines 2 and 3 could be changed to achieve the following effect:

Another way to develop the melody, is to add extra notes. For example, here, some auxiliary notes (*) and some passing notes (+) have been added:

The finished composition can be written in several ways. For example, the melody can be written on a single stave with indications to the performers when to begin:

Alternatively, the finished composition could be set out on three separate staves in one of two ways. In Figure 13.1a, it is written in a rather concise way, suggesting that all performers start in turn with the top stave of music. A tempo mark, dynamics and title have been added. A lengthier but perhaps clearer way of setting out this composition is illustrated in Figure 13.1b. Each instrument is given its own stave.

Figure 13.1 a and b   a   *Canon for 3 Glockenspiels*

b   *Canon for 3 Glockenspiels*

If we number the bars in the above canon (six bars to each statement of the melody), the completed manuscript would look like this:

Glockenspiel I   1   2   3   4   ‖: 5   6   1   2   3   4   :‖

Glockenspiel II   1   2   ‖: 3   4   5   6   1   2   :‖

Glockenspiel III   ‖: 1   2   3   4   5   6   :‖

If you wish to produce a round, the rhythm and mood of words may provide ideas for your melody. It is, therefore, probably best to find the words first. Simple poems, epigrams or limericks, for example, can be most effective. However, it is also possible to compose the melody first, and then add the words, if you prefer to work that way.

Figure 13.2 is an example of a canon for three B♭ clarinets, composed by the method which has been described above. Each instrument, starting with Clarinet 1, performs in turn from the beginning. Each instrument then follows eight bars behind the previous performer. The composition may be repeated as many times as the performers agree.

Figure 13.2   *Clarinet Trio: Turnaround*   C. Binns

ASSIGNMENTS

1 Choose some rounds to perform. Sing them with a group of friends and then perform the rounds on suitable instruments. You may choose like-instruments, such as three glockenspiel or three flutes, or you may choose three different instruments, such as violin, recorder and oboe. Do not forget to transpose any part to be performed by a transposing instrument such as the B♭ trumpet or Horn in F. You may like to begin with *Three Blind Mice*.

Figure 13.3   *Three Blind Mice*   (original in Ravenscroft's Deuteromelia, 1609)

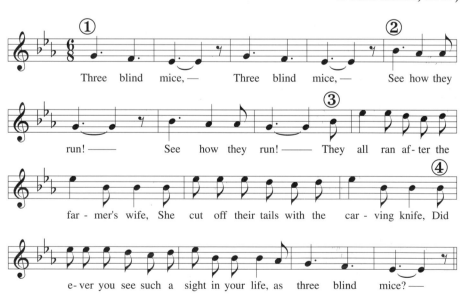

2 Compose a round for three voices. Write out, perform and record your composition.

3 Compose a canon at the unison for three instruments. Write out, perform and record your composition. Do not forget to transpose any part which will be performed by a transposing instrument.

Other types of canon

There are many different types of canon. Although so far, we have looked at **canons at the unison** (where all the voices enter at the same pitch), the imitating voice may enter at a different pitch. Often, for example, the imitating voice may enter a fifth higher, (**canon at the fifth**) or a fourth lower than the first voice. The vocal canon *Non Nobis, Domine*, attributed to the English composer William Byrd (1543–1623), is shown in Figure 13.4. It is presented in three parts, with the second voice pitched a fourth below the first voice, and the third voice pitched one octave below the first voice.

Non Nobis, Domine   William Byrd   *Figure 13.4*

William Byrd (1543–1623)

Figure 13.4 Non Nobis, Domine (continued)

Other types of canon include:

Canon Two in One: A canon for two voices, each voice performing the same melody in turn.

Canon Three in One: A canon for three voices, each voice performing the same melody in turn.

Canon Four in Two or **Double Canon**: Four voices performing two canons simultaneously. Each canon is sung by two voices.

Canon by Augmentation: The melody given out by the imitative voice is in longer notes, double the value of the first voice.

Canon by Diminution: The melody given out by the imitative voice is in shorter notes, half the value of the first voice.

Canon by Inversion: The intervals by which the melody proceeds in the imitative part are inverted. Hence, an upward interval in the melody becomes a downward interval in the imitative part.

Retrograde Canon or **Canon Cancrizans** (**Crab-Canon**): the imitative part presents the melody performed backwards.

SUMMARY ASSIGNMENTS

1 Find an example of two different types of canon and write brief notes about each. If possible, listen to a recording of each canon and perform the music with some friends.

2 Choose one type of canon from the above list and compose your own canon for voices or instruments. Write out, perform and record your composition.

14

Pentatonic music, music built on the whole-tone scale and modal music

Pentatonic music

The pentatonic scale

The pentatonic scale can be found in the music of many cultures including those of China, Polynesia, Japan, Africa, India, the American Indians, the Celts and the Scots. The scale consists of five different notes and can begin on any note. It contains no semitone intervals and can be illustrated by using notes:

(a) C, D, E, G, A (C), or (b) C, D, F, G, A (C)

or on the keyboard by playing the black notes only. For example,

(c) C#, D#, F#, G#, A#, (C#) or

(d) F#, G#, A#, C#, D#, (F#)

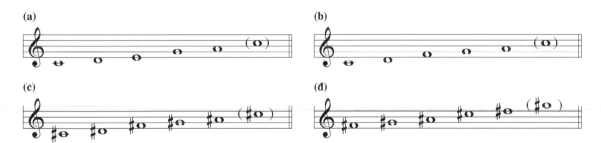

Pentatonic melody

Melodies constructed using only the notes of a pentatonic scale have a particular beauty and quality. Figure 14.1a is an example of a melody built upon the pentatonic scale using the notes F, G, A, C and D.

Slowly

mf

Figure 14.1a

ASSIGNMENTS

1 Compose an eight-bar pentatonic melody for an instrument of your choice.
Perform and record your composition.

2 Compose a 16-bar pentatonic melody for an instrument of your choice.
Perform and record your composition.

3 Compose a pentatonic vocal melody, adding words of your own. Perform and
record your composition.

Accompaniment to pentatonic melodies

Accompaniment to pentatonic melodies can be provided either by adding
suitable chords or by choosing an accompaniment that is itself built upon
the pentatonic scale. Ostinato patterns and drones also provide an effective
accompaniment to a pentatonic melody. The pentatonic melody (Figure
14.1b) is shown with added chords.

Figure 14.1b

The same melody is shown in Figure 14.1c, but this time the
accompaniment consists of a one-bar ostinato pattern built on the same
pentatonic scale which we used for the melody. The composition could be
played on an electronic keyboard by one or two performers, or it could be
performed on two different instruments such as violin (upper part) and
cello (lower part).

Figure 14.1c

This composition could be presented in many different ways. For example,
the upper part could easily become the lower part by transposing it down
one octave. The lower part could then become the upper part by
transposing it up two octaves. In other words, the parts simply change
over as in Figure 14.1d.

Figure 14.1d

ASSIGNMENTS

1 Compose a pentatonic melody and add an accompaniment. Your music may be for one instrument (such as a piano or electronic keyboard) or for two instruments (such as two flutes, violin and guitar, or oboe and bassoon). Write out your composition and then perform and record it.

2 Compose a pentatonic ostinato and then add a pentatonic melody. You could work on your own, either performing both parts of the music yourself (on a piano or electronic keyboard, or by recording the ostinato part on tape which can be replayed as you perform the melody). You could also work with a friend, each performing one part of your composition.

Improvised pentatonic music

Because of the nature of the pentatonic scale it is impossible to create harsh dissonances, even if several people are improvising at the same time. Provided that all the players use the same pentatonic scale, group improvisations often work well, particularly on tuned percussion such as glockenspiels and xylophones. A combination of ostinato patterns and improvised melodies can work very effectively.

Another approach to pentatonic improvisation is for each member of the group to choose a different pentatonic scale. The outcome may not always be successful, but occasionally it will be very exciting.

ASSIGNMENTS

1 Choose one pentatonic scale as the basis for a group improvisation. Work together and experiment with this pentatonic scale, discussing ideas as you try them out. Organise your music into a composition to be performed by the group.

2 Working as a group, select a pentatonic scale and devise an ostinato which can be performed by one or more instruments. As some members of the group perform the ostinato the remaining members should each take a turn to improvise a melody. You may wish to record all the music, and then listen to your work on tape and discuss the results. This will help you to consider any changes or improvements which could be made to the composition before making a final recording.

3 In a group, work on a pentatonic composition for a small number of instruments and explore the possibilities of combining long sounds and short sounds. For example, you could devise an ostinato (perhaps consisting only of long sounds, or alternatively, consisting only of short sounds), which could be performed while other instruments add a pentatonic melody or melodies. Consider the dynamics of your composition, deciding how loud or how quiet each part should be. Write out your composition or record a performance of your music.

Music built on the whole-tone scale

Music built on the whole-tone scale has a special vague, atmospheric and unearthly quality. Many composers have written effective and beautiful music based on this scale. The whole-tone scale was particularly used by group of French composers called the *Impressionists* and included Claude Achille Debussy (1862-1918). The whole-tone scale, as the name suggests, consists only of intervals of a tone. Only two versions of the scale are commonly used: one beginning on the note C, and the other beginning on C # (or Db). The first four bars of a simple melody based on the whole-tone scale built on the note C, is shown in Figure 14.2a.

Accompaniment to whole-tone melodies

There are several ways to add an accompaniment to a whole-tone melody. A very simple method would be to take single notes from the whole tone scale and add them as a lower part. Alternatively one or two notes repeated in the lower part will produce a drone or pedal point. In Figure 14.2b, the note C, doubled at the octave, is repeated through each bar to give a sustained and somewhat ominous effect to the music.

A more adventurous accompaniment can be made by taking several notes from the whole-tone scale and arranging them into chords. The accompaniment in Figure 14.2c was composed in this way. A title and some performance instructions have been added.

Figure 14.2a, b, c

ASSIGNMENTS

1 Listen to some of Debussy's music and write brief notes about your choice. His
work includes the piano pieces *La Cathédrale Engloutie*, *Jardins sous la pluie*, two
Arabesques and the suite *Children's Corner*. His orchestral music includes
Images, *La Mer*, *Nocturnes* and *Prélude à l'après-midi d'un faune*. In particular,
you may like to choose *Voiles* from Debussy's first book of *Préludes*. This
composition is written almost entirely in a whole tone scale.

2 Compose a melody built upon a whole-tone scale. Select a suitable instrument
to perform your music and write out or record the composition. Give your
composition a suitable title.

3 Compose a melody built upon the whole-tone scale and add a suitable
accompaniment. Your composition may be for a keyboard instrument or for an
instrument with keyboard accompaniment. Give your composition a title, and
write out or record your music.

Modal music

The modes were early forms of scales, which dominated European music
for over one thousand years up to the sixteenth century. Only then did
their influence gradually begin to decline. There were four fundamental or
authentic modes, each containing eight notes. Each authentic mode began
on a different note (D, E, F or G). The organisation of the notes in the
scale or mode (all corresponding to the white notes of a keyboard
instrument), determined that each of these modes had a different
arrangement of tones and semitones.

The four authentic modes, **Dorian, Phrygian, Lydian** and **Mixolydian**,
are shown below. Each **authentic** mode had a **plagal** form which began on
the fifth degree of the authentic. The plagal modes were called
Hypodorian, Hypophrygian, Hypolydian and **Hypomixolydian**. To
these modes were added the **Aeolian** and **Hypoaeolian** modes and the
Ionian and **Hypoionian** modes.

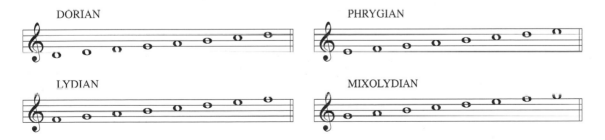

Modal compositions have a distinctive quality about them. Figure 14.3 is a
composition based on the notes of Dorian mode for unaccompanied
saxophone.

Figure 14.3   *In Distant Mode*   (for Eb Alto Saxophone)

C Binns

SUMMARY ASSIGNMENTS

1 Play the melody *In Distant Mode* (Figure 14.3), on a suitable instrument. You do not have to use a saxophone.

2 To the melody *In Distant Mode*:

  a add a drone bass. If the instruments performing the melody and the drone bass are both non-transposing instruments, the drone bass should be the note D (below middle C). For example, the melody could be performed in the written key by violin, with the drone bass on the note D, given to an electronic keyboard or bowed double bass. If one or both instruments are transposing instruments, transpose the music accordingly.

  b add a drone consisting of the two notes D and A (below middle C), like this:

    Select a suitable instrument to perform the drone.

  c add a bass part using only the notes D, C and B♭ (below middle C). (The note B♭ is not found in the Dorian mode, but works well as part of an accompaniment to this piece. You will find that the note B, which is part of the Dorian mode, has not been used in this melody.) Here are the notes you may use:

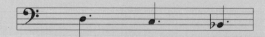

Experiment with these three notes to find the most effective way of using them. You may use any appropriate time value for each note. Select a suitable instrument to perform the bass part.

   d add some chords to be performed on piano, electronic keyboard or guitar. You may choose any chords, but those of D minor, C major, B♭ major and A minor will be effective.

3 Compare the four accompanied versions of the music you composed in question 2. Comment upon each piece and the effect produced by the addition of each lower part.

4 Compose an instrumental or vocal melody in one of the modes and give the music a suitable title. Perform and record your composition.

5 Compose a modal melody for any instrument or voice and add some accompaniment. The accompaniment may be played on the same instrument (if you are working on a keyboard instrument) or on a different instrument. Perform and record your composition, and give the music a title.

15
Images, drama and music

Pictures, photographs, paintings and images can be a valuable source of inspiration for the composer. An endless supply of images can be found in books, magazines and newspapers, and virtually any image can be taken as a starting point for a composition. Sometimes, an image, such as a photograph of people, animals, objects or places, will provide a stimulus and suggest an obvious theme for a composition. The music which it inspires is descriptive and the composer's response to the image is quite apparent from the character and title of the music. You could also focus upon a particular detail or aspect of an image, making this the starting point for your composition. Sometimes, your response to an image may produce a composition, the theme of which is quite contrary to that of the image.

ASSIGNMENT

Find a photograph, painting or image to use as a starting point for a composition. Your music does not necessarily have to describe the image, but must have some connection with it. When completed, record your composition, which may be for one or any number of instruments and voices.

Hector Berlioz (1803–1869)

Programme music

During the nineteenth century descriptive pieces, called **programme music**, became fashionable. Composers often tried to create moods and suggest images in their music, which reflected places, people, emotions, events or stories. Some well-known descriptive or programmatic pieces of music include:

Mendelssohn: *Hebrides Overture*

Berlioz: *Symphonie Fantastique*

Prokofiev: *Peter and the Wolf*

Mussorgsky: *Pictures at an Exhibition*

Dukas: *The Sorcerer's Apprentice*

Saint-Saëns: *Danse Macabre* and *Carnival of Animals*

Smetana: *Vltava* (from *Ma Vlast*)

Honegger: *Pacific 231*

ASSIGNMENTS

1 Study and listen to one piece of descriptive or programme music. Identify the scene, incident, emotion, experience or story which the music is trying to convey, and write about how the composer achieves this.

2 Compose and record a piece of descriptive music for one or more instruments, giving your composition an appropriate title.

Music and advertisements

Television advertisements nearly always aim to combine images and music to promote the products which they are selling. These adverts employ a wide range of styles of music, although pop music and classical music are used most frequently. Sometimes, the music in the advert is a song, or **jingle**, which features the name of the product. Alternatively, appropriate instrumental music is used, setting a mood or reflecting the quality of the item being advertised. Television adverts have to get their message across in a very short space of time. Many provide excellent examples of how to combine images and music in a very effective way.

ASSIGNMENTS

1 Make a list of ten different television adverts, all of which feature music. For each advert, comment on the images and music used, and say why you think that the advertisers have chosen to present the product in the way that they have. State how important the music is to the advert. (Would an alternative piece of music be equally effective?) Say how successful you think the advert is.

2 Working on your own or in a group, compose some music for a television advert. You may choose to compose some alternative music for an advert that is currently on television, or you may invent your own product to advertise. Your music may be a song or an instrumental composition. Record your music.

Film music

Film music provides another combination of pictures and music. It is written to create atmosphere and to emphasise and enhance the visual image. There is a great deal of excellent film music from which you could learn much about suspense, atmosphere and emotion in music. In the hands of a skilled composer, the combination of appropriate music and interesting visual images can be very powerful indeed. While you may not

Ralph Vaughan Williams
(1872–1958)

have the opportunity to compose music for a film, there may, however, be opportunities to experiment with your own 'film' music if you have access to a video camera and play-back equipment.

ASSIGNMENTS

1 Listen to some film music and discuss the role and importance of the music to the film. You could start with *Star Wars* (Williams), *Dr Zhivago* (Jarre), *Henry V* (Walton) or *Scott of the Antarctic* (Vaughan Williams).

2 Working in a group, produce a short video with a soundtrack.

Incidental music

Music occurring in the spoken play is called incidental music.

Just as music can enhance the visual impact of a film, music may also make an important contribution to stage plays and dramatic performances. Incidental music dates from Greek drama and the liturgical plays of the Middle Ages. The plays of Shakespeare and Molière occasionally require incidental music, and the composers Purcell, Beethoven, Mendelssohn, Bizet and Grieg have all composed such music.

Incidental music may be performed before the stage drama begins (**overture**), between the acts or between two scenes (**entr'acte music**, **interlude** or **intermezzo**), or during the course of a scene. The music may represent the on-stage characters or their actions, set the mood of a scene, or provide music that may be required in the play such as a dance or a song. It may be scored for any number of instrumentalists to perform 'live' during the drama. Alternatively, the music may be pre-recorded and played on tape, or performed using computer-linked equipment if this is more appropriate.

Edvard Grieg (1843–1907)

ASSIGNMENTS

1 Find an example of some incidental music. Name the dramatic work in which it features, the author of the work, and the composer of the music. Write brief notes about the music, and describe its particular role in this dramatic work.

2 Compose a piece of incidental music which could be used at a particular point in a play or dramatic presentation. Choose a play with which you are familiar or look for opportunities to compose music for your school play or local drama group production. You could compose an overture to be performed before the play begins, or music which sets the mood of a scene. Alternatively, your composition could be performed as background accompaniment to a monologue, or dialogue. You could also compose music to represent the main characters or dramatic themes. Additionally, there may be opportunities to compose music for a ceremony, procession, dance or song if any occurs in the play. If you compose several pieces of music for the play, they could be arranged as a suite for concert performance.

Opera, operetta and musicals

In opera, operetta and musicals, the visual impact, the dramatic elements and the musical content combine to produce memorable, moving and sometimes spectacular moments. Ideally, you should experience all these aspects live in the theatre or opera house as the composer (and author or librettist) intended. If this is not possible, you could watch opera, operetta and musicals on television, video and film, or listen to sound recordings of the music.

There may also be opportunities for you to join a school production, or local dramatic or operatic society, either on stage or as a member of the orchestra or band.

*Giacomo Puccini
(1858–1924)*

SUMMARY ASSIGNMENTS

1 Write about any opera, operetta or musical which you have seen in the theatre, briefly describing the story, and those aspects which you particularly enjoyed.

2 Below are a few well-known operas, operettas and film and stage musicals. Listen to excerpts from one of the following, and find out as much as you can about the work which you have chosen.

The Magic Flute (Mozart)
Madame Butterfly (Puccini)
Carmen (Bizet)
Die Fledermaus (Strauss)
Orpheus in the Underworld (Offenbach)
The Pirates of Penzance (Gilbert and Sullivan)
The Music Man (Willson)
West Side Story (Bernstein)
Kiss Me, Kate (Porter)
Phantom of the Opera (Lloyd Webber)
Les Misérables (Boublil and Schönberg)

*Jacques Offenbach
(1819–1880)*

16
Music by chance

The art of composing music is a curious mixture of skills, experience, inspiration and, occasionally, luck! Few of us embarking upon a new composition can be absolutely sure of the outcome. Although the finished composition is the product of many different influences, most of them are under control. There are, however, many ways of composing and performing music which rely far more heavily upon the element of chance.

Improvisation

Improvisation means making up the music as you go along, producing something which is unpractised and spontaneous.

Improvisation (sometimes called **extemporisation**) is an important skill for both the composer and the performer, although it is less evident today than in previous centuries. Musicians in J S Bach's time (called the Baroque period), were trained in the art of improvisation and would freely extemporise at the keyboard. Singers, too, would readily improvise, adding extra notes, embellishments and ornamentation to the written vocal music which they were performing. Occasionally, improvisation produces outstanding music, and some composers, particularly J S Bach, Handel, Mozart, Beethoven, Mendelssohn and Liszt, became as famous for their skilful improvising as they were for their written compositions. Sometimes, composers would improvise together, occasionally competing with each other, as in the meeting between Mozart and Clementi in Vienna in 1781.

Figured bass was a system of musical shorthand, using figures and signs written below the bass notes in a single line of music.

One aspect of improvisation important during the seventeenth and eighteenth centuries was the realisation (or performance) of a **figured bass** (also called **thorough bass** or **basso continuo**).

The figures and signs indicated the required harmonies, which were not written out in full, by giving the intervals of the other notes above the bass note. While the bass part in the ensemble was often played on bass viol, cello or bassoon, the harmonies were filled in by a *continuo* instrument which could play chords, such as the harpsichord or organ.

It was, however, often unnecessary to add figures to every note; for example, common chords in root position were not figured, except where one of the notes required an accidental before it. While the harmonies were indicated, decisions about exactly how to realise the figured bass (such as the distribution and arrangement of the notes in each chord) were left to the imagination and musicianship of the performer. Here are some examples:

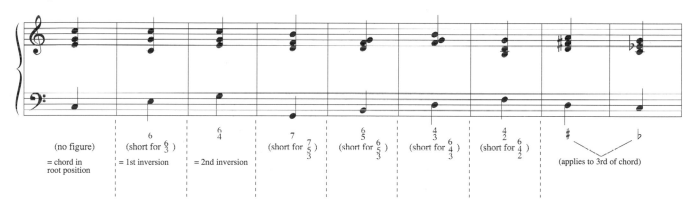

As well as providing the chords indicated by the figured bass, the performer would frequently add decoration and ornamentation to the part. Nowadays, the continuo part of works originally written with a figured bass, is written out in full for the keyboard performer.

To find out more about figured bass, ask your teacher for suggestions about further information and listening.

Another aspect of improvisation often occurred in the *concerto*.

If you have heard any concertos, you will know that towards the end of some movements (usually the first movement) the orchestra stops playing and leaves the soloist to perform alone, often producing a dazzling display of technical skill. This point in the concerto is called the **cadenza** and the performer, particularly during the Classical period, would improvise, playing any appropriate music that came to mind. Many composers often performed their own music, playing the solo instrumental part themselves, and would freely improvise a cadenza. Occasionally, the solo performer in a concerto was not the composer, but was nevertheless still expected to provide an improvised cadenza. In this way, the performer became a joint composer. Today, most concertos include a written cadenza for the soloist to learn; not many performers would risk improvising.

Although improvisation is less apparent than in the Baroque and Classical period, it still remains an important element of some types or styles of music. For example, improvisation is an important ingredient of Indian classical music, and is fundamental to jazz, blues and American country music. Some pop musicians, singers and church organists are highly accomplished in this art.

Improvisation and the composer

Improvisation has considerable significance for the composer. The practice of working at the keyboard, or any other instrument, experimenting with sounds and exploring ideas is a valuable method of composing. Often, improvisation does not throw up startling ideas but, occasionally, an exciting theme or some harmony will appear, which can then be further expanded and developed. Improvisation is not, however, something which you should attempt in a hurry, nor is it something to try in a noisy or crowded room.

Start with an idea, perhaps using some chords or part of a melody, and try to develop it. Take your time, experiment and don't worry if the outcome is not always entirely successful. Jot down good ideas or tape your improvisations, and then analyse what you've done and identify aspects for future development. You will find that the more you improvise, the better you'll become at it. In the following Assignments are some musical themes upon which you can improvise.

ASSIGNMENTS

1 Using an instrument of your choice, or your voice, improvise around any of the ideas in Figure 16.1. Try to develop a piece of music from one of them. The final result may be quite unlike any of the given starting ideas.

Figure 16.1 Ideas for improvising

2 Listen to a concerto of your choice and identify where a cadenza occurs. You may use a miniature score to help in this task. Write brief notes about the cadenza, mentioning at least four points of interest about this feature of the music. Your teacher may help you to select a suitable concerto, should you so wish.

3 Listen to one piece of jazz, identifying as far as possible where improvisation occurs. Write about the music, giving as much information as you can. Mention, for example, the names of the performers, the instruments or voices used, the style of jazz and the role of improvisation in the music.

Interpretation

All music requires the performer to make decisions of interpretation; that is, deciding how the music should be played. It is, of course, very useful if the composer writes detailed performance instructions on the musical score, indicating precisely what is required in terms of speed, phrasing and dynamics, for example. Some written music, however, gives very few clues to the performer about the composer's intentions, other than providing the actual pitch and rhythm of the notes.

Music written at the time of Corelli (1653–1713) and Handel (1685–1759), for instance, did not always include written instructions about aspects of performance, such as the intended ornamentation. This was often left to the performer's discretion.

Sometimes, performance details in musical scores are omitted by editors who recognise that some earlier printed editions of music have not always been a true representation of the composer's instructions. In such cases, it is often thought better to omit performance details altogether, as the composer's original intentions are now unknown.

Figure 16.2a, for example, is a composition for solo trumpet, but with the phrasing, speed and dynamics deliberately omitted. How accurately do you think a trumpeter could perform this music? Could the composer complain if it was not just what he or she had in mind? To ensure that the performer knows the composer's exact intentions for this composition, the information in Figure 16.2b could be added.

Even when there is a detailed score of the music available, the performer's interpretation of the music may vary somewhat with each performance. If

Figure 16.2 a and b

the same piece of music is performed by another musician, the interpretation may be quite different. One of the problems is that words are not always very precise in their meaning. Take a simple example. The term **allegro** means 'quick and lively', but is somewhat imprecise, since we can not determine exactly how quick 'quick' is. Even with an added metronome mark (e.g. Allegro ♩ = 138), there is no guarantee that the performers will play the music at the exact tempo suggested by the composer. There are many fierce arguments about musical interpretation, with each performer aiming to give what he or she thinks is the most accurate performance.

ASSIGNMENTS

1 Compare two recorded performances of the same piece of music with the same, or different, performers. You may choose any type of music. Write about the differences and similarities of the two performances, and explain any preference you may have for one of the performances.

2 Compose a melody which can be performed by a friend. Choose a suitable instrument and write out your music. You could, for example, compose a 16-bar melody for flute. Make a copy of your composition and add to it performance details such as speed, phrasing, articulation and dynamics.

Ask your friend to perform your composition using the score which contains no performance details, but aiming to give a musical and thoughtful performance of your music. You may wish to record this performance.

Compare this performance with your marked score and notice how the two are similar and/or different. Write brief notes about your findings.

Aleatory music

Aleatory music, or **music by chance**, is an exciting way of composing and performing music. It involves elements chosen at random, by the composer or the performers, resulting in music which has not been totally pre-determined by the composer. One of the first composers to use aleatory elements was Charles Ives (1874–1954), followed by Henry Cowell (1897–1966) and John Cage (1912–1992). There are many ways to introduce the element of chance into the process of composition, and some ideas are given here.

Dice music

In dice music the composer sets the rules by which the composition will be written, but then allows chance to take over and determine the final outcome.

- Two people each have a die. One die will represent the pitch of the notes and one will represent rhythms. For example: Die 1. The six numbers will represent notes:

A   B   C   E   F# D   (You may choose any notes)

1   2   3   4   5   6

- Select a time signature, perhaps $\frac{4}{4}$, and choose some note values which would 'fit' into such a time signature. For example, in $\frac{4}{4}$ you will often see ♩ and ♪

- Allocate your note values to numbers like this:

Die 2 ♩   ♩   ♩   ♩   ♩   ♩

          1   2   3   4   5   6

Charles Ives (1874–1954)

- Decide how many throws of the dice you will make; for a start, let's say 16 throws. Each person throws his or her die and makes a note of the numbers. For example, the first throw could produce a 5 from die 1 and a 2 from die 2. Looking at the chart, on die 1, number 5 represents the note F♯, and on die 2, number 2 represents ♩

So, on manuscript paper you would write this:

- Carry on until you have each had 16 throws (or as many as you want). Subsequent compositions may involve hundreds of throws!

An example of a dice composition produced by two people using the above method, follows. One person determined the pitch of the notes, while the other was responsible for the rhythm. Each person was allowed 16 throws of the die.

Die 1 - (Pitch)   Throws: 2 6 1 1 5 4 5 2 6 3 3 4 1 5 2 1

Die 2 - (Rhythm) Throws: 3 2 4 4 6 1 3 2 1 4 2 6 5 2 1 6

Looking back to the chart organised earlier, this would produce the following result:

Die 1 - B D A A F♯ E B D C C E A F♯ B A

Die 2 - ♩ ♩ ♩ ♩ ♩ ♩ ♩ ♩ ♩ ♩ ♩ ♩ ♩ ♩ ♩ ♩

John Cage (1912–1992)

Write this onto manuscript paper. If you have a bar which does not add up (for example, in ($\frac{4}{4}$) ♩ ♩ ♩ will not fit), either change the time signature for that bar ($\frac{5}{4}$) or change one of the notes to fit the time signature. For example, ♩ ♩ ♩ could become ♩ ♩ ♩ to fit in $\frac{4}{4}$.

You may also choose a tempo and some dynamics using chance methods. For example, one roll of the die could determine the tempo, like this:

1 Allegro	4 Lento
2 Largo	5 Presto
3 Moderato	6 Vivace

Dynamics could be decided like this:

1 f	4 mp
2 pp	5 cresc.
3 mf	6 dim.

You will still have to decide where to place these dynamics or you may prefer to look at the piece and choose your own dynamics instead. Give the composition a title and select a suitable instrument to play the music. The outcome of the above example of a dice music composition is shown in figure 16.3.

There are many other aspects which could be explored using the dice method of working. Rests, for example, could be added at the throw of a die. You could increase the range and number of notes by using several dice. This method could also be used to compose music for more than one

The Sad Violin (Violin)   **Figure 16.3**

instrument, such as a duet, trio or quartet. However you produce your aleatory music, you must always listen carefully to the final composition. Pieces produced in this way are not always successful or predictable, so be prepared for an outcome that could disappoint or delight.

ASSIGNMENT

Working on your own, or with a friend, experiment with dice music and produce a composition using this method. Perform and record your music.

Variations on a dice theme

As an alternative to the dice method of composition, random numbers upon which to base your composition may be generated by a computer, for example. You could also simply number pieces of paper or write different notes on the paper, fold them up, and then choose them at random. How about organising a group of friends to take turns saying the first number (up to 8) which they think of? Make sure that someone writes the numbers down, or tape records this process. There are many different and original ways of producing chance music. One rather novel method, for example, uses darts and a dartboard. To each number on the board is allocated a pitch or time value for a note. While this method of composition may instantly appeal to darts players, a serious word of caution: *whether you are working at school or at home, please get permission to try this particular approach, so as to avoid any potentially dangerous method of composition*. The idea is to produce music, not hospital cases!

ASSIGNMENT

Working on your own or in a group, devise a method of composing music in which the element of chance plays an important role. Experiment with your method, produce a composition and record the results. Make a second attempt at the composition, using the same method. Compare the two compositions.

Performance by chance

Imagine giving a score to a performer, or group of performers, which deliberately omits instructions and is intentionally vague in its meaning. In these circumstances, the performer has to make many more decisions about the interpretation and outcome of the music score. The composer has less control over the end result, and becomes an organiser or enabler, while the performer becomes a joint composer. The music score for the performers can be written as notes on a stave, in your own invented notation, in words or in pictures. Figure 16.4 shows three examples.

Figure 16.4

Hysteria (Horn in F)

The Hedgehogs (Duet for 2 Xylophones)

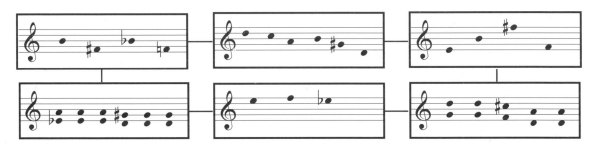

Could you improvise a piece of music from this picture score? Do you think that it really is a score?

On the Pier
(Quartet for B♭ Clarinet, B♭ Trumpet, Glockenspiel and Snare Drum)

This type of composition is great fun to organise and to perform. It is a good idea to have a tape recorder ready to record the outcome, as the same score will prompt many different interpretations. There is, however, one small problem with this area of composition. Unless the work is realised, you may be exposed to criticism about the effectiveness of your score. Taken to the extreme, you could present your performers with a blank piece of paper and allow them total freedom of interpretation. Whatever your score looks like, it is the end result, the music, which is important.

If you are submitting work of this nature for an examination, you must provide the examiner with a recording of the composition. If you only submit a piece of paper with scribbled hieroglyphics, or a photograph of a carrot without the recorded music, an examiner might assume that you are not taking the examination seriously.

SUMMARY ASSIGNMENTS

1 Two composers who have produced music containing chance elements are John Cage and Karlheinz Stockhausen. Find information about these composers and listen to some of their music. Your teacher will be able to help if you require assistance with this.

Write about one of the pieces which you have listened to, state how it is organised and describe the effectiveness of the music.

2 Organise a performance and recording of one, or more, of the three scores in this section: *Hysteria*, *The Hedgehogs* and *On the Pier*. If you do not have the instruments which are specified, you may choose alternative instruments to realise the score.

Work in a group and discuss the results.

3 Produce a score which can be freely interpreted by a soloist or group of performers. The score may take any form you wish. Record the performance of your music, and discuss the outcome with your performers.

17

Simple arrangements

An arrangement is the adaptation of a piece of music to be performed by an instrument, group of instruments, voice or voices, other than originally intended by the composer.

Some arrangements, or **transcriptions**, such as piano arrangements of symphonies, overtures and other large-scale works, are based strictly upon the original music. In such cases, the arranger does not add any new material to the original music, and simply produces an alternative score which contains only the music of the composer. This type of arrangement is also found in vocal scores (for example, of opera, operetta, musicals and oratorio) where the orchestral parts are arranged for piano rather than written out in full.

A piano reduction is a musical score where the orchestral parts have been arranged for piano.

Other arrangements involve a much freer and more creative adaptation of the original music, and may include many additions and modifications. A skilled arranger can produce brilliant and exciting results, and there are countless examples of excellent arrangements for all kinds of ensembles. However, to arrange music well takes time and much practice.

If you are going to arrange a piece of music it is important to know something about the instruments or voices for which you intend to write. Be particularly aware of the range of notes and the quality of sound each can produce. It may be necessary to consider the skill of the performer, especially if the music is to be played by a beginner instrumentalist. Try to develop the skill of 'mentally hearing' what you write and imagine the sound of each instrument or voice which you require. For example, imagine the following theme

- played by a violin.
- played by clarinet.
- played by a trumpet.
- sung to 'la'.

Many great composers have written fine arrangements of either their own, or other composers' music. You too can choose whether or not to arrange your own music or borrow from another composer. When you are preparing to make an arrangement, write for the resources available, so that you are assured of hearing your music performed. Arrange some music to be played by your friends, by a school ensemble, or by a band or group to which you belong.

Duets

The opening bars of a keyboard composition, shown in Figure 17.1a, could be used as the source material for an arrangement. As this music is written on two staves, one possible approach is to consider an arrangement for two instruments, allocating the music on each stave to an instrument.

The choice of an instrument to perform the music on the upper stave does not present any real problems. There are many instruments which could play the part. The lower part might be problematic. It is too low for some instruments (such as the flute or oboe), while for others it could be difficult to play, or not suit the characteristics of that instrument (such as a trombone or tuba). There are, however, several instruments ideally suited to the realisation of this part. If wood-wind performers were available, the lower part could be performed by a bassoon and the upper part by an oboe. This would sound particularly effective. Each instrument could play the music without any alteration to the original, other than the addition of articulation marks if required.

If resources were available, instead of using two solo instruments, this two-part arrangement could be performed by two groups of like-instruments such as violins (upper part) and cellos (lower part). When you have completed the full score (that means the score showing the full

a   *In the Nick of Time*   C L Avier

Moderato

mp

etc.

Figure 17.1 a and b

b   *In the Nick of Time*   C L Avier
Arranged for Oboe and Bassoon by C Binns

Moderato

Oboe

mp

Bassoon

sempre stacc.   *etc.*

arrangement for all the instruments), either give a copy of this to each performer or write out each individual part. Usually, in larger ensembles, each performer only has a copy of his or her own part.

ASSIGNMENT

Find a composition for piano or a keyboard instrument written on two staves but with only two parts (for example, some beginner piano music, or one of J S Bach's *Two-part Inventions*). Arrange the music for two instruments, or two groups of like-instruments, and organise a performance of your own arrangement. If your preferred instruments are not available, perform both parts of your arrangement on an electronic keyboard instrument using appropriate voicings.

Trios

Music originally written in two parts can often be arranged for more than just two solo performers, or two groups of performers. Sometimes, a third part can be produced without inventing any new material, by simply allocating some of the notes from the original music to a third instrument or voice. In Figure 17.1, the opening bar of the lower part looked like this:

Instead of allocating this part to one instrument (such as the bassoon), the part could be divided between two instruments in either of the following ways:

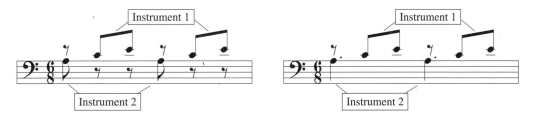

The three parts together (with the 'new' part written in the treble clef) would then look like this:

If the additional part was allocated to B♭ clarinet, the music would have to be transposed. The opening bar of the woodwind trio would look like this:

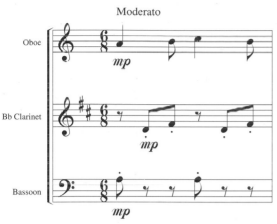

Just as a two-part keyboard composition can readily become the source material for an arrangement for two instruments or voices, so too can a three-part keyboard composition become a trio for three instruments or voices. As an example, the trio in Figure 17.2 could be arranged for three violins or three clarinets, or if the key, or clef, was unsuitable, then the whole piece could be transposed to a more appropriate pitch. Three trombones, for example, could give an exciting sound. You do not have to choose three like-instruments. The trio would sound as effective with two trumpets and a French horn, or two violins and a viola. The possibilities are endless.

Figure 17.2

ASSIGNMENT

Find a composition in three parts for piano or a keyboard instrument. Arrange the music for three instruments, or three groups of like-instruments, and organise a performance of your arrangement. If your preferred instruments are not available, you could perform each part of your arrangement separately on an electronic keyboard instrument, selecting an appropriate voicing and record your work using a multi-track recorder.

Quartets

Quartets allow for an even greater choice of instruments. Figure 17.3a shows the first eight bars of a hymn tune, written in four parts. It could easily be arranged for a group of four instruments. In examples b and c the music has been arranged for string quartet, and also for brass quartet. Each part has simply been given to an instrument, and no new material has been added at all:

Figures 17.3 a, b and c

a   *Ferndale*   C Binns

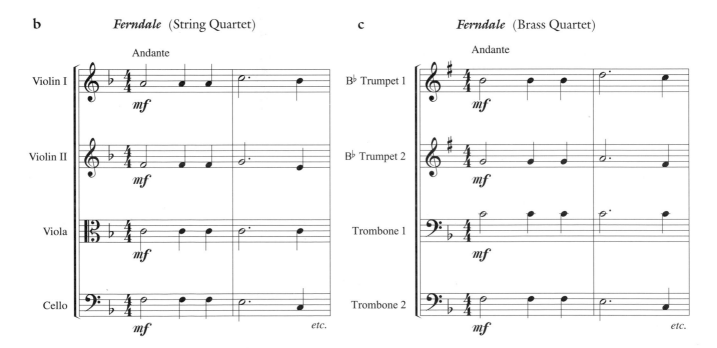

b   *Ferndale* (String Quartet)

c   *Ferndale* (Brass Quartet)

ASSIGNMENT

Using a composition in four parts for piano, electronic keyboard or voices (such as a hymn), create an arrangement for four instruments, or four groups of like-instruments. If your preferred instruments are not available, you could perform each part of your arrangement separately on an electronic keyboard instrument using an appropriate voicing and record your work using a multi-track recorder.

Extra parts for more instruments

There are several ways in which extra parts for additional instruments or voices may be added to an arrangement.

1 Allocate two or more like-instruments to each part.

This simply means that a part for one instrument or voice is duplicated so that a group of instruments or voices can perform the same part. The composer does not need to create any additional music. For example, a part for one violin can be performed by any number of violins.

2 Allocate one part to two or more different instruments.

Just as one part can be performed by any number of like instruments, so too can one part be allocated to two or more different instruments. For example, the four written parts of the quartet *Ferndale* could be allocated to a variety of brass instruments which could then all perform together:

Part 1 : E♭ soprano cornet, B♭ cornet, B♭ flugelhorn
Part 2 : B♭ cornet, E♭ tenor horn, B♭ trombone
Part 3 : E♭ tenor horn, B♭ baritone, B♭ trombone
Part 4 : B♭ euphonium, bass trombone, B♭ bass, E♭ bass

Some parts would have to be transposed, although every part would be based entirely on the original quartet. No new music would be added.

3 Allocate notes, or sections of the music, to an additional instrument or voice.

This procedure does not involve the creation of new musical material, but is rather a re-allocation of the parts already available. For example, as we have seen earlier, the duet *In the Nick of Time* was arranged as a trio by allocating part of the music to a third instrument.

4 Allocate a part to be performed by one or more additional instruments at a pitch one or two octaves higher or lower than the original.

For example, the oboe part in the duet *In the Nick of Time* could be performed by a flute, one octave higher than the oboe part. The additional part can be performed simultaneously with the original part (the oboe part in this instance), or can alternate with the original, as in Figure 17.4.

Figure 17.4

In the Nick of Time

C L Avier
Arranged for Woodwind Trio by C Binns

5 Add new ideas to the original music.

The addition of new material to produce an arrangement involves a considerable knowledge of harmony and instrumentation. To produce a large-scale arrangement requires much work and effort. This should not in any way discourage you, as the skill of arranging applies not only to your arrangements of the music of other composers, but also to arranging and organising your own compositions. It is not possible here to provide all the information for creating original and effective arrangements. However, you can learn much by studying arrangements wherever possible. There is a great variety of music for you to investigate, including music for solo instruments such as the piano or guitar, and music for band, orchestra and choir.

Arrangements and scoring for large ensembles

When you compose or arrange music for a large ensemble, you will have to consider carefully how to allocate the music to each voice or instrument. If you are working on an original composition, one method is to notate your music firstly as a melody with added chord symbols and some performance details, like this:

Figure 17.5

Melody for M B from *Concert Rock* (for Concert Wind Band)

C Binns

This type of score provides a useful reference from which you can then make a detailed condensed score (see also page 212) showing how the music will be organised and allocated, like this:

Figure 17.6 Melody for MB condensed score

You will now have sufficient information from which to produce a full score.

Summary

1 Always study the original music carefully before starting to make your arrangement.

2 Decide which instruments or voices will perform your arrangement, checking their range and the key and character of the music.

3 Always produce a first draft of the arrangement, and check it carefully for accuracy and effectiveness. When arranging music for a larger ensemble, consider making a condensed score to show how the music will be allocated to each voice or instrument. Do not be too eager to complete your work until you are satisfied with the result.

4 Write out the full score as neatly as possible, showing clearly which instruments or voices are required, and including any performance details such as tempo, dynamics, phrasing and articulation. If the arrangement is intended for a small group, you may copy this score for each performer. If the arrangement is for a larger ensemble you should write out the individual parts as well as your full score.

5 Always acknowledge the composer if the arrangement is not of your own music. This means that you should write the composer's name at the top of the full score and on any individual parts which you write. In some cases, you may only make an arrangement of someone else's music with permission. If in doubt, ask your teacher. If you are still in doubt, avoid it!

6 Organise a performance of your arrangement.

You should ask your teacher for guidance about the laws of copyright which protect the rights and interests of fellow composers.

SUMMARY ASSIGNMENT

Listen to an arrangement for a large ensemble such as a band, orchestra or choir, and, if possible, study a score of the music. Alternatively, you may be a member of a band, orchestra or choir which has performed an arrangement. Your conductor may be able to provide you with a score. Look at the ways in which the music is presented, and how the arrangement is organised and developed. If you can, refer to the original music and compare the two versions. Write about your findings.

18
Presentation

The way in which you write your music is very important. Examine the extract below. A list of questions immediately springs to mind:

Duet   N V Good

- Which instruments should we choose? The composer has not given any information about this. Perhaps two recorders, or oboe and violin?

- Does Part 1 start before Part 2? Because of the way in which the parts are written, it looks like it should.

- What tempo does the composer intend?

- Why are there no indications of dynamics?

- Part 2 does not have a key signature while Part 1 does. Is this an omission, or is it intentional? Are the Fs in Part 2 meant to be F or F#?

- Part 2 has not been given a time signature. Presumably, it is the same as for Part 1, or is it different?

- Are there really two minims in bar 3 of the Part 2? Is this intentional, or a misprint?

- Why, in bar 2 of Part 2, are the note stems written downwards?

- The bar lines are not in line with each other. (They are not aligned correctly.) Is this intentional?

Each player might attempt to perform his or her own part, but anyone looking at this 'full' score would certainly become confused. The composer probably knew exactly what he or she wanted, but was not very good at communicating this information.

Even though you may occasionally prefer not to write your music down or may use a computer and printer to produce a very accurate score, you quite often will want to handwrite your own scores. If you choose to do so, you must make them as neat, accurate and as easy to understand as possible.

Jottings

Many composers work at the piano or with a keyboard instrument, trying out ideas and experimenting with sounds. If you choose to work in this way, jot down any ideas as they occur, using a pencil and an eraser. Try out many possibilities until you are satisfied with the result. Only when the process of composition is complete is it time to write a neat score, showing exactly what you want.

The neat copy

If your composition is for one performer, especially if you are also the performer, you may only need one copy of the music. However, it is a good idea to make a photocopy of your manuscript, just in case you misplace the original.

If your composition is for a group of performers, you will either have to give a copy of the full score (all the parts together) to each performer or, if the music is for a large ensemble, write out individual parts for each performer. Figure 18.1 shows the opening bars of a string trio written in full score, but also including individual parts for each performer.

If the music is likely to be rehearsed or performed many times, make a photocopy of each part and keep the original. Give the copies to the performers, then if a part is lost you will always have the master copies for reference. Photocopying will take time and can be expensive, but it may save you some trouble. If it is your own composition (music and words), you may copy and photocopy as often as you wish. If it is someone else's music or words, you may not copy without permission.

Manuscript paper

For most purposes the normal twelve-stave paper is ideal. Compositions for band, orchestra and large ensembles involving many parts require manuscript paper with more staves. You can buy larger-sized manuscript paper (for example, containing eighteen or twenty-four staves). Some paper is available with the names of instruments and appropriate clefs already printed.

If you cannot find suitable manuscript paper, you can always draw the staves by hand. You can use a special five-nibbed pen, although it can be a bit messy to use. This type of pen does, however, provide an inexpensive alternative to buying manuscript paper.

FULL SCORE

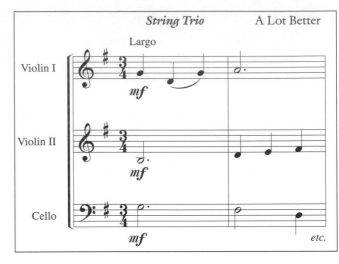

INDIVIDUAL PARTS

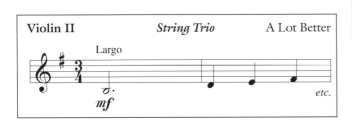

Figure 18.1 String Trio: full score and individual parts

When using manuscript paper, select white manuscript with bold black lines. This will photocopy best. The cream-coloured paper is often of a good quality but is less suitable for photocopying. On some types of manuscript paper, the five lines are not printed too well and cheaper paper tends to blot with ink pens.

What to write with

Final copies always look best when written in black ink. It photocopies well, whereas pencil and some blue inks do not. Most printed music has notes written accurately and evenly. Trying to copy this style of presentation, however, would be difficult and time-consuming. Printing techniques are not the same as handwriting techniques. For your music writing, you need a pen with a nib which will produce thick (—) and thin (|) strokes. A biro or ball point will not do. A fairly broad pen nib is most useful. Calligraphy pens are quite good, as are certain art pens and special 'music' pens. You could buy the old-fashioned kind of dip pen with a broad nib, and a bottle of black ink. These are inexpensive and, with practice, you can produce excellent results. However, until you get used to it, this type of pen can be very messy!

The ideal pen for students is probably a simple fountain pen with a fairly broad nib and black ink or ink cartridges. You should aim to write neatly, accurately and quickly. Your musical handwriting can be as distinctive as your own handwriting, but you will have to practise to perfect your own style.

If you are left-handed you may have greater problems with an ink pen, trying not to smudge your manuscript work. 'Left-handed' pens may not help much either. The only solution is to practise and persevere until you find a style that suits you. It is worth the effort!

Handwriting

As well as writing your musical notation neatly, you should also aim to present your script as neatly as possible when adding words to your scores. For example, you will need to give your composition a title, name the composer and put in any acknowledgments or dedication at the top of the page. (This does not always happen, but occasionally pieces are dedicated to particular people, performers, places or events.) You should name the instrument required and write in the tempo. Clefs, key signature, time signature, dynamic marks and phrasing should also be added, although you may consider these to be part of your music notation skills.

If the composition is a song, you will also have to add the words. For handwriting, you may choose your 'music' pen (with the broad nib), a fountain pen with a medium or fine nib, a rollerball-type pen, a fine felt-tipped pen, or a drawing pen with a steel point.

Try to write in the same style every time. Do not change styles of handwriting in the middle of a composition.

Other equipment

As well as manuscript paper, pen, ink, pencil and eraser, you will also need a ruler. This is essential for drawing bar-lines which pass through more than one stave, and will also help you to check **alignment** (see page 148). You will need a long ruler for completing scores with bar-lines which may pass through many staves.

If you are using an ink pen, a sheet of blotting paper may also be necessary.

ASSIGNMENT

Copy the extracts from Figure 18.2, as accurately as possible, onto manuscript paper. Take care to make the stems of notes perfectly upright and the notes themselves of a uniform size, correctly spaced. If you are working in a group you could compare and discuss your results,

Figure 18.2 Extracts to copy

Lettering

For a really professional-looking finish you can use dry transfers for titles, name of composer and dedications, but transfers are expensive. For a good alternative, try using a stencil which will also produce neat, uniform lettering. Alternatively, practise your handwriting, until you can produce neatly-written titles.

Alignment

Alignment refers to the placement of music notation on the stave to show exactly which notes or rests in one part occur simultaneously with notes or rests in other parts.

If more than one part of your music is written on a single stave, or parts are written on more than one stave, such as piano music, or music for a duet, trio or quartet, it is very important to align the written parts correctly. In other words, your score should show exactly when different parts should play (or be silent) together. A score which is not aligned correctly is very difficult to read. Compare example **a** with example **b** in Figure 18.3. Looking at the second example, you cannot really tell when the parts play together.

You can learn a lot about alignment from studying printed scores of music. In Figure 18.4, the *Air* from Bach's *Suite no.3 in D*, the parts are correctly aligned, and it is quite clear how they all fit together.

a (correct)   Allegro

Figure 18.3 Alignment

b (incorrect)   Allegro

Figure 18.4   *Air* from *Suite no 3 in D*   J S Bach

Spacing

It is important that you space your music out correctly, considering the following two aspects:

- Organise each written bar of your music carefully, so that notes are spaced to allow for ease of reading. A general rule to follow is that, in the same bar, notes of greater time value should be spaced more widely than those of lesser value. For example, in Figure 18.5, example **a** is easier to read, and therefore more 'correct' than example **b**.

Figure 18.5a and b

In some instances, you will have to give notes or rests a little more space than is normally allowed. This may happen when there is more than one part to the music. For example, if one part contains many notes in a bar, while another part occurring at the same time has fewer notes, the latter may have to be spaced more widely than usual, as in Figure 18.5c.

Figure 18.5c

Notes often have to be spaced a little wider than usual when setting music with words for voices. In such music, the length of each word and the time value of the notes, will dictate the spacing. The following example, Figure 18.6, shows how more space is required when words are added to the melody.

Figure 18.6

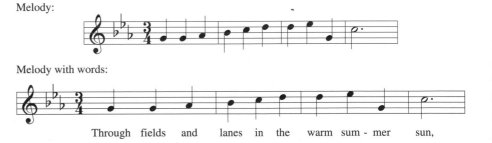

- Think carefully about the number of staves and pages of manuscript paper which will be required when writing out your composition. For example, if your music needs to be written on two sides of manuscript paper in order to be read clearly, you should not try to squash all the composition onto just one side of the paper. If you are writing a single-line melody which keeps fairly well within the five lines of the stave, then use all the staves on the paper. If, however, there are lots of ledger lines which cannot be avoided, it is sometimes best to miss out every other stave, otherwise the music can become very difficult to read. (Where the notes use a succession of ledger lines, try using the **8ve** sign or, in some cases, change clef.)

The following example, in Figure 18.7a, requires no ledger lines, and although some performance details have been added to the score, the music can easily be written on successive staves.

Figure 18.7a and b

If the same music were written one octave higher (Figure 18.7b), it would be easier to write the part on alternate staves, to allow sufficient room for the ledger lines and the performance details.

The practice of leaving alternate blank staves in hand-written scores is quite acceptable, since the manuscript paper is already printed and the size of the gap between each stave cannot be increased. In professionally printed scores, the space between the staves may be adjusted according to printing specifications. Occasionally, when writing your music on every stave (without leaving alternate blank staves) you may not have sufficient room in one particular place to add performance instructions. For example, this happens in band or orchestral parts, when there are a number of simultaneous performance instructions, or there is a change of key or tempo which does not coincide with the beginning of a new stave. By moving onto the next stave, the problem as shown in example **a** is easily solved, as shown in example **b** of Figure 18.8.

Figure 18.8a and b

Organising your score

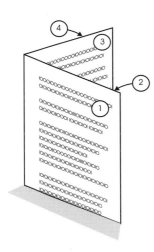

If your music fills a double sheet of manuscript paper, and you intend to give this to the performer (rather than a photocopy of your music), write on the two sides of the manuscript paper which do not need a page turn. Write on pages 4 and 1 (in that order) or 2 and 3 (in that order). Leave the other two sides blank. You may consider this a waste of paper, but it often does help the performer.

Rehearsal letters and numbers

If your composition is of any great length, it is useful to mark each section with a letter or a number. This helps the conductor and performers to identify exact bars in the music without excessive counting.

While these reference points may occur at regular intervals in the music (such as every eight, 12 or 16 bars), they frequently do not appear with such regularity. Usually, they mark the beginning of a section, a change of key or a change of tempo. Rehearsal letters should be written in bold capitals and may be framed by a square or circle, as shown below.

Page turns

If your composition is more than one page long, think carefully about the page turns. Do not write your music in such a way that the performer has to turn the page in the middle of a passage. Try to organise your score so that the page turn coincides with performers' rests or the end of a movement. It may be necessary to leave several staves blank in order to have a sensible page turn. Also, be aware that some instruments will require a little more time for a page turn than others. If a quick page turn is unavoidable, warn the performer by writing **V.S.** on the manuscript, in the lower right-hand corner.

V.S. (volti subito) means turn over the page immediately.

Count the bars

If you have been copying music out from a rough score, or writing orchestral or band parts from a full score, always check that you have written the correct number of bars. It is very easy to miss out a bar. For scores with lots of instruments, make a simple checklist like the one in Figure 18.9, and cross-check with the individual parts to ensure that no bars have been missed out.

Figure 18.9

CHECKLIST	
Savile Park Suite (First Movement)	
SECTION	NUMBER OF BARS
Beginning to A	4
A to B	16 (including repeat)
B to C	8
C to D	8
D to E	5
E to F	8
F to G	8
G to End	10

Mistakes

It will be unusual if you do not make some mistakes in the actual writing out of your composition. If mistakes occur in rough work, it is not a problem. However in your finished manuscript, it is never advisable just to cross out mistakes. They should always be removed completely, using one of the following solutions:

Liquid paper

Simply paint over the mistake with liquid paper. The liquid dries in seconds and you can write over the top of it. The spirit-based type of liquid paper is highly flammable and, like white paint, if you spill it on your clothes or on the carpet, you may have a difficult job of removing it. It can also give off harmful fumes. The water-based type of liquid paper is much safer to use.

Scissors and glue

Cut out a new piece of manuscript like the one on which you have made a mistake, and glue the new paper in place to cover the error. Depending on the type of glue you use, be careful not to write on a soggy new piece of manuscript paper, or your work will blot. Normally, when the music is photocopied, it is almost impossible to detect where the mistake is.

Start again

As a last resort, if the mistakes are too numerous, start again and re-write the page.

To achieve a neat, well-presented score will take time and practice. It is highly likely, however, that you will gain a great deal of personal satisfaction from careful attempts, and the completed manuscript will certainly be appreciated by all who perform your music.

SUMMARY ASSIGNMENT

Find copies of printed music and study the layout and presentation. Make a list of the features which illustrate good practice, such as accurate alignment, easy-to-read notation and clear instructions for the performer. Note the positioning of the title, the composer's name, tempo, expression marks, dynamic and phrase marks.

19

Music for cardboard boxes and imagination

The rather odd title for this chapter was prompted by the performance of an inspired composition which featured, among other things, cardboard boxes played as a drum kit. The composition used different timbres (qualities of sounds) by drumming on the empty boxes, and included rhythm patterns drummed on parts of an old washing machine. The composition was extremely effective.

Though we live in a highly technological era, compositions of the cardboard box variety highlight the fact that you do not necessarily need expensive equipment to produce successful compositions. The extent of your equipment and resources matters little if you do not use one of the composer's most valuable resources: imagination. As a composer you are trying to communicate with your performers and your audience and the music should provoke a reaction.

Wherever possible, experiment with your compositions, try new approaches and be adventurous in your work. Listen to as much music as possible, and always be self-critical until you achieve the best result.

Composing is a real skill. It takes a long time and a lot of effort to develop fully. It also means making occasional mistakes. If you persevere, you will begin to produce compositions of real quality and flair. Not only will you feel a sense of achievement, but your music will give pleasure to others as well. Figure 19.1 shows a composition for three performers, using everyday objects. Perhaps it will give you some ideas for your own work.

SUMMARY ASSIGNMENTS

1 With two friends, organise a performance of *Percussive Paraphernalia*. Try to use the suggested instruments, but if these are not readily available, choose others which will be equally effective.

2 Compose a piece of music for a number of everyday (safe) objects. You may perform all the parts yourself, or involve others in the realisation of your music. You do not have to write out your composition, but if other performers are involved, you will have to explain to them exactly what you require. Finally, record the composition.

Percussive paraphernalia (Trio for empty tin can, wooden chair and metal wheelbarrow)   C Binns

Figure 19.1 Percussive
paraphernalia

20
Composition checklist

Having completed a composition, it is important to check that every detail is correct. You may also wish to write out a neat copy of your music, add an annotation and record the music. The following checklist should help to ensure that nothing has been overlooked in the preparation and presentation of your work, and that the finished product is as accurate as possible.

1 Always listen to your music and be guided by the sounds you hear. The process of composing should never be a theoretical exercise, completed in silence without reference to the real music. Experienced musicians can imagine sounds and compose without an instrument, but this approach is not recommended to the student. It is, however, a skill which will develop with practice.

2 Always perform the composition, or ask other musicians to perform it. Record the results and, again, listen critically. Be prepared to change details of your composition if you are not satisfied with the outcome. Always review and revise the music if necessary.

3 Written compositions should be neat, accurate and legible. The following points should be taken into account:

• Have you given your music a title and written it on the score?

• Have you written your name on the composition?

• If the music is an arrangement, or variations on another composer's theme, have you acknowledged the composer?

• Are you including a dedication (to a person, situation, ensemble, etc.) on the score?

• Have you written the names of the instruments or voices for which the music is composed?

• Does every stave begin with a suitable clef (𝄡 𝄢 𝄞)?

• If you have put a key signature, does it appear as it should, on every stave following the clef ?

• Have you included a time signature written after the clef and key signature at the beginning of the music? If the time signature does not change throughout the piece, it should only appear once at the beginning. If the time signature changes, you should add the new time signature in the appropiate places. At the beginning of your music, the order is clef, key signature, time signature. An easy way to remember this is to note the alphabetical order C–K–T.

- Have you put a tempo mark at the begining of the piece? You may use Italian or English terms (or French or German if appropriate) such as **lento** (very slow), **moderato** (at a moderate speed) or **prestissimo** (as fast as possible).

- Have you given an indication of the character of the music, using terms such as **agitato** (agitated), **dolce** (sweetly), or **maestoso** (majestically)?

- Are all notes and rests written correctly? Check note stems, position of rests and spacing of notes.

- If there are any accidentals, do they appear before the note to which they refer? (For example ♯♩ , and not ♩♯)

- Does every bar add up to the correct number of beats and are notes grouped correctly?

- Have you written bar-lines in the correct places (and not omitted one at the end of a stave, for example)? Have you finished with a double bar-line ?

- Have you added dynamic markings to your music, such as *pp*(very quiet), *p* (quiet), *mp* (moderately quiet), *mf* (moderately loud), *f* (loud), *ff* (very loud), $<$ (gradually louder) and $>$ (gradually quieter)?

- Have you added expression marks and marks of accentuation such as ♩ (accent), ♩ (staccato) and ⌢ (slur)?

- Have you written phrase marks over the music? Are they required?

- Have you indicated performance details or special effects particular to the instruments for which you are writing? For example:
  Stringed instruments: add bowing marks and effects such as **pizzicato** or **con sordino**
  Brass instruments: use of mute and tongued or slurred notes
  Woodwind instruments: tongued or slurred notes
  Percussion instruments: choice of beaters, sticks, brushes, mallets
  Piano: pedal markings
  Electronic keyboard: voicings, automatic drum rhythm, single-finger function

- If you have composed some vocal music, have you written the words (or syllables) under the notes to which they refer?

- If the composition is for an instrument, is the music playable? Always keep within the instrument's range, checking that the clef is correct and that the key you have chosen is suitable for the instrument. Vocal music should keep within the vocal ranges. If in doubt, refer to the *Rudiments and Reference* section, or ask your teacher.

- When writing music for transposing instruments, always check your transpositions carefully, especially if there are several different transposing instruments. Will all the instruments sound in the same key?

- If you have written out instrumental or vocal parts, copying from your full score, have you checked that all the parts have the same number of bars as the original? Have you numbered the bars and included rehearsal letters or numbers?

- Is the music aligned correctly?

- Have you written exactly what you mean?

- Do you need to take a photocopy of your music?

4 If you are writing an **annotation** or **commentary** to accompany your music, particularly for an examination, does it include the following information and details:

- Brief description of the music, including the equipment which you have used?

- Form and structure?

- Composing process, including any help given by others?

- Recording techniques?

5 If you have recorded your music, is your tape:

- Organised, so that your recording is easily found?

- Well recorded?

- Clearly labelled, with details also on the tape insert card?

- Mixed-down, if originally recorded on a four-track machine?

- If you have produced a score in addition to a taped realisation of your work, is the music exactly the same in both? If there are discrepancies between the written score and the recording, you should explain this, stating which version is the 'correct' one.

21
Composing for examinations

This chapter gives advice about the preparation and presentation of your compositions for the GCSE music examination, along with information about how compositions are assessed. Some of the words connected with examinations may be new to you, and you may wish to refer to the *Glossary*, or explanation of words used in connection with examination, at the end of this chapter. It may be helpful for you to go through the glossary with your teacher who can answer any questions you may have.

Some things you should know

Although each Examination Board has its own particular requirements for GCSE Composing, there are many aspects connected with preparation, presentation and assessment which apply to all GCSE music examinations, regardless of which GCSE music syllabus you follow. It is important to establish which Examination Board you will be entered for and which syllabus you are following. The Examination Board may have more than one music syllabus. Your teacher will have this information and may provide you with a syllabus, or part of the syllabus, to help you prepare for the examination.

Examination preparation

Your compositions for the GCSE examination are described as 'coursework', as you have produced them over a period of time. There are no Examination Board rules about the exact length of time which you should spend preparing your compositions, although most candidates for the GCSE Music examination will have produced their work during a two-year course. The amount of time spent preparing for the examination will depend upon your own circumstances. If you are following a GCSE course at school, your teacher will give you guidance about **when** to produce your compositions. There are many different approaches to this, and there is no one 'correct' way to prepare. For example, your teacher may ask you for compositions at regular intervals, perhaps one each term, or one each half term. Alternatively, your teacher may only request compositions from you later in the course, when you have had time to experiment and develop your composing skills.

Whether you are preparing for the examination at school, college or as a private candidate, you must plan ahead and think about organisation, so that you can complete your work on time. Three important points to remember are:

1 Find out the final date by which you must hand in your finished compositions.

2 Plan your time, and have some idea about how and when you intend to produce your work for the examination.

3 Do not under-estimate the length of time it may take to complete a composition. If you intend to record, notate or annotate your work, give yourself plenty of time to do this. You cannot hope to produce all your compositions in the last few days before the final deadline!

What to produce for the examination

The examination syllabus will provide all the necessary information about what you have to produce. While each Examination Board has different requirements, all GCSE music examinations aim to assess a candidate's ability to compose or arrange music in a traditional and/or a contemporary idiom. The examination looks to reward positive achievement in candidates. This means that marks are awarded for what you know, understand and can do.

What style of composition shall I choose?

There is much freedom of choice about the style and presentation of your compositions, and no one particular style of composition will gain you more marks than any other. It is the quality of your work that is important. Some Examination Boards provide suggestions about the type of compositions that you might produce, although the choice is left to you. While the list below is not exhaustive, most candidates present one or more of the following compositions:

- An instrumental composition for a solo instrument, with or without accompaniment, a duet, trio, quartet, or music for a small instrumental ensemble.

- Vocal music, such as a pop song, folk song, carol, hymn, blues or part song.

- A piece composed in a stated form, such as binary, ternary, rondo and variation.

- A march, fanfare or a dance such as a waltz, jig or gavotte.

- A piece featuring a structural element such as a drone, ostinato or round.

- A composition written in a particular style or demonstrating a particular technique such as Impressionism, serialism, minimalism or aleatory music.

- Music for electronic keyboard.

- Music using technology such as multi-track recording, sequencer or computer.

- Music reflecting influences of non-European cultures, such as Afro-Caribbean, Asian and Oriental.

- Music for an occasion.

- Programme music, or a piece based on a chosen theme or mood.

- Incidental music, or music to enhance or interact with another medium or media such as dance, drama, video or the spoken word.

- An arrangement of a piece for instrumentalists or singers.

What qualities should my composition demonstrate?

It is not possible to produce one set of guidelines which would provide you with information about particular qualities that every composition should demonstrate. Different styles of music have different qualities, and what is important in one piece of music is not always as relevant in another. However, the Examination Board music syllabus will provide details of what is called the 'assessment (or marking) criteria for composing', which is a list of qualities and skills which will be considered, where appropriate, when your work is marked.

Assessment criteria vary with each Examination Board, but here is a general list of the qualities mentioned most frequently. Some, although not necessarily all of the following points will apply to your composition.

- A clear sense of wholeness, balance, scale, structure, control and organisation of ideas.

- Understanding of instruments, voices or sound sources.

- Use of form.

- Melodic shape, control, appropriateness, flow, ornamentation, phrase length, sequence or repetition.

- Control of rhythm, tempo, tonality, dynamics, accompaniment and harmonic aspects.

- Technical knowledge.

- A sense of mood, appropriate to the title or words of the piece.

- A sense of style which is maintained throughout the piece.

- Development of material.

- Clear performance details.

- Use of appropriate or effective texture, layering, density or colouration.

- Accurate notation or annotation, appropriate to the music composed.

- Originality, resourcefulness, imagination, impact, effectiveness and success.
- The ability to communicate your ideas to listeners.

How many compositions do I have to produce?

The demands of each examination syllabus are different, and you are advised to check exactly how many compositions are required. Some examinations require a certain number of pieces (for example, two, three or four), or state the minimum requirement. Others suggest an approximate playing time, such as five minutes.

Careful selection of the pieces submitted for examination is important, and you should discuss this aspect with your teacher. Wherever possible, it is important to provide variety within your submission. Avoid including too many compositions of a similar style, since they rarely gain additional marks. A single composition, unless it is substantial, will probably not allow a candidate to demonstrate a range of composing skills.

Presentation

While your music will be judged on how it sounds, it is important to present any written score or annotation as clearly and as accurately as possible. You will find advice on the written presentation of your music in Chapter 18, *Presentation*.

Keep all your written work neat and legible. Label all your work clearly, including scores, annotations and tapes with your name and the name of your centre. Graphic scores should include a key to the symbols used, and music of an experimental or aleatory nature must give clear instructions to the performers.

Taped realisation

A taped realisation is a recording of your music. In many cases, you will be allowed to perform your own composition and tape record your music. If your music is written for more than one performer, you will have to ask others to help you, or multi-track the different parts yourself.

If you intend to include a taped realisation of your music for the examination, where other performers are involved, it is important that they follow your instructions about how to perform your music. They should not add anything extra to your music, unless this is your intention. They must not change, add to or improve any part of the music, as the composition cannot be assessed as all your own.

In some music, such as a piece composed by more than one person, the contribution of others to the composition and performance of the music is quite acceptable, but you must be able to show clearly who has done what. For example, if you have composed a piece for a rock group, but the drummer has composed or improvised the drum part entirely on his or her own, you must acknowledge this in your annotation or declaration form.

A taped realisation is always very useful for the assessor, who can actually hear what you intended. In some cases, a taped realisation is essential, particularly if you have submitted a graphic score or a piece of an experimental or aleatory nature.

If the taped performance of a written composition is not perfect, do not worry. You will not be penalised.

Annotation or Commentary

A written score usually provides sufficient information about your music to the assessor. A taped realisation enhances the score. If you are submitting a taped realisation without a score, an annotation or commentary is essential.

An annotation is a written explanation about your composition, stating **what** you did and **how** you did it. It should provide as much relevant information as possible, and give the assessor clear details of your intentions and the composing process. A good annotation could include the following:

1 Brief description

This should include the title of the piece, the keys (or mode), time signature, tempi and basic structure. State the instrumental and/or vocal resources and any influences you may have had in composing the music.

2 Form and structure

Outline the form and structure of your piece in detail, including any song words if appropriate. Note down any chord progressions used. If your piece uses a compositional device such as a riff or ostinato, try to write out a few bars of this and include it in the manuscript. If the piece has a graphic score, explain the signs and symbols you have used, and say why you have used them. Draw a chart to outline the overall structure of the piece, pointing out important elements such as key changes, and changes of instrument and/or voices, rhythm and tempo.

3 Composing process

Explain clearly how the piece was composed. Write detailed notes about any instruments used in composing the piece, including computers and software. If the composition is the result of group work, say how this was done and explain your role. State exactly what you have done. Acknowledge any assistance which you may have had from your teachers or other persons.

4 Recording techniques

State how the piece was recorded, including who was involved. If other performers were involved in the realisation of your music, and you have not written a score, you must explain how they knew what to play. If you have used multi-track equipment, state which parts were recorded

first and why. If you have used a sequencer or computer, give details of
what you have done.

Check that your annotation is as accurate as possible, and sign and date it.

Authentication and declaration

All Examination Boards require that the compositions you submit for the
examination are 'authentic', meaning that they are your own work. Group
compositions are allowed, but each person's contribution must be
identified.

If you have used the work of others as a starting point for a composition or
for an arrangement, you must give details of this. You and your teacher
may have to sign a form stating that your compositions are your own
unaided work. Any help which you have received must also be declared.
Your teacher is also responsible for informing you about the Examination
Board's rules and regulations concerning authentication.

**Authentication is very important. Never include the work of others in
your folio without declaring it. The consequences could be very
serious.**

Glossary of examination words

Annotation: A written explanation about your composition, stating what
you did and how you did it.

Assessor: A person who assesses, or marks, your compositions.

Authentication: The compositions which you submit for the examination
must be authentic, that is, your own work. While it is quite acceptable
to use the music of another composer as a basis for your own work
(perhaps Variations on a well-known melody, or an arrangement of
someone else's music), you **must** declare this, and state which part is
your work and which part is not. Any help which you have received
must also be declared.

Candidate: A person taking an examination or a test.

Commentary: A written explanation about your composition; like an
annotation.

Commissioned composition: For examination purposes, a commissioned
composition is one which you have produced having worked from a
given stimulus provided by the Examination Board. For example, a
poem, piece of prose, photograph, scenario or opening theme is given,
upon which you have to base a composition.

Component: A part or aspect of something more complex. The word is
used in connection with examinations to mean a particular part of the
whole examination. For example, the 'Composing component' simply
means the composing part of the examination, as separate from the
'Performing' or 'Listening' components.

Coursework: The compositions which you complete in preparation for the examination.

Declaration: A written statement that your compositions are your own unaided work. If you have received help, you must also provide details of this. The Examination Board will probably provide you with a form to fill in, which has to be signed by you and your teacher.

Examiner: A person who inspects and marks an examination.

Folio: A collection, or group of compositions. For examination, you will have to submit a folio of your compositions.

Marking criteria: Rules and guidance about how compositions should be assessed, and the standards upon which marking is based. Details of marking criteria are usually explained in the syllabus.

Moderator: A person who moderates, marks or checks work submitted for an examination. A moderator also checks standards, and ensures that all candidates have been assessed accurately.

Realisation: When this term is used in connection with the GCSE music examination, a 'realisation' means that you have made your composition 'real' in sound by performing it. For examination purposes, the performance should be recorded making a 'taped realisation', in other words, a taped recording of your compositions. This should be supported by a written score or annotation of each piece.

Score: The written presentation of your music. A score contains information about your composition, and can be written in musical notation, words, tablature, chord symbols, or presented graphically as a **graphic score**, using symbols or illustrations.

A **full score** shows each individual part in music composed for more than one performer. When a number of parts are written in a condensed version, it is called **short score**.

Source material: Any written text, such as a poem, article or story, musical score, or recording, image or photograph which you have used as a starting point or as a basis to produce your own composition. For examination work, you should include a copy of any source material in your folio.

Syllabus: The syllabus is a booklet provided by the Examination Board which tells you exactly what is required for the examination.

22
Rudiments and Reference

The stave

This is a stave:

A stave (or staff) consists of five lines, on which the music is written. Notes are written on a line or in a space like this:

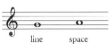

and each note is given a letter name.

The musical alphabet uses the first seven letters A B C D E F G, and these are repeated when required. Each stave must begin with a clef.

The treble clef or G clef

This is a treble clef:

It fixes the exact pitch of the second line up as the note G above middle C. (See page 168)

A treble clef is used when music is written for higher voices and instruments such as the violin, clarinet, flute and glockenspiel. The treble clef is also used for high notes on the piano and nearly all brass band instruments.

If a note is placed on every line and space of the stave (here we use one called a semibreve), with a treble clef at the beginning, the letter names of the notes are as follows:

A good way to remember the letter names and position of the five notes E, G, B, D and F on the lines in the treble clef is to learn the saying **Every Green Bus Drives Fast**:

The four spaces in the treble clef spell **F A C E**:

The bass clef or F clef

The bass clef can be written like this:

or this:

It fixes the exact pitch of the fourth line up as the note F below middle C. Dots are always placed on either side of the F-line when writing the bass clef. A bass clef is used when music is written for lower voices, low notes on the piano, and for the lower range of such instruments as the bassoon, cello and double bass.

If a note is placed on every line and space of the stave (here we use one called a semibreve), with a bass clef at the beginning, the letter names of the notes are as follows:

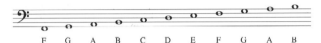

A good way to remember the names and position of the five notes G B D F A on the lines in the bass clef is to learn the saying **Green Buses Drive Fast Always**:

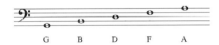

The four spaces A C E G in the bass clef can be remembered with the saying **All Cows Eat Grass**:

The keyboard

Most keyboards (such as a piano, organ or synthesizer keyboard) don't have the names of the notes written on them, so they look like this:

You will have to learn where the notes are on the keyboard in order to play your music. While the white notes on the keyboard are side by side, the black notes are placed in a regular pattern of three black notes, a gap, and then two black notes. Start by learning the names of the white notes, as shown on this section of a keyboard:

Each note has its own special place on the keyboard. The black notes act as a guide, so that, for example, the note D is always between two black notes, while the note B is just to the right of the three black notes. This diagram shows you how to find notes on the keyboard with notes written in the treble and bass clefs. Ledger lines (see page 174) have been used.

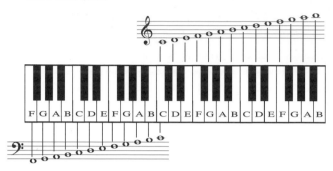

This note in the middle of the keyboard is called middle C. It is also written in the middle between the two staves.

It can look like this:

or this:

Often in piano music the two staves are joined together with this sign { called a brace. Notes are arranged as follows:

Tones and semitones

The smallest distance, or **interval**, between any two keys (or notes) on a keyboard is called a **semitone**. It is the distance between any one note and the nearest note to it, above or below, black or white.

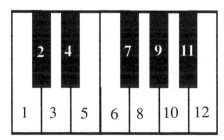

For example, on the keyboard illustrated here, the interval between notes 1 and 2 is a semitone, as is the interval between notes 2 and 3, 3 and 4, and 5 and 6. The word semitone means half-tone. A **tone** (or whole tone) is equal to two semitones. For example, the interval between notes 1 and 3 is a tone, as is the interval between 2 and 4, 4 and 6,

and 5 and 7. On the stave, a tone is always found on the next line if the first note is in a space, or in the next space if the first note is on a line.

 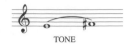

Sharps, flats and naturals

This is a sharp: ♯ It raises a note one semitone in pitch.
This is flat: ♭ It lowers a note one semitone in pitch.
This is a natural: ♮ It restores a note to its original pitch.
To explain about sharps and flats, look at the keyboard below with all the notes named.

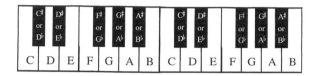

Find the note F. Now look at the black note just to the right of F. As this note is one semitone higher than F it is called **F sharp**. However, it also has another name. As it is one semitone lower than G we can call it **G flat.** Whether you choose to call a note sharp or flat will depend upon the **key** you are in. Keys are explained later. We would write F sharp like this:

The sharp sign comes before the note, and is always written on the same line or space as the note to which it refers. It warns us that the following note is to be raised one semitone. Although we say 'F sharp', we actually write 'sharp F' on the stave.

Similarly, a flat lowers a note by one semitone. The flat sign comes before the note, and is always written on the same line or space as the note to which it refers. G flat is written like this:

When we want to return a note which has been a sharp or flat to its original pitch, we place a natural sign in front of the note to show that it is neither a sharp nor a flat note:

Accidentals

Accidentals are **sharps**, **flats** or **naturals** which occur in a piece of music, but are **not** included in the **key signature** (see page 176). Key signatures refer to sharps and flats placed at the beginning of the music to indicate the key of the music.

Once an accidental appears, it affects only the bar in which it is written. (Bars and bar-lines are explained on page 170.) In the following example all the Fs in bar 1 are F sharps. In bar 2, the last note is F natural, while bar 3 shows how to write F sharps and F natural within the same bar.

Little Blues

Time values

A clef helps us identify the letter name of a note on the stave, and its pitch (how high or low it is), but it does not tell us how long the note lasts for. The length of the notes is identified by using the following time values or note values.

- ○ semibreve or whole note
- ♩ minim or half note
- ♩ crotchet or quarter note
- ♪ quaver or eighth note
- ♬ semiquaver or sixteenth note

A semibreve is twice as long as a minim; a minim is twice as long as a crotchet; a crotchet is twice as long as a quaver; a quaver is twice as long as a semiquaver.

Other note values seen less frequently include the **breve**, written as |o| or |o|. It is twice as long as a semibreve and is rarely used now. The **demisemiquaver** or **thirty-second note** ♪ is half as long as a semiquaver. The **hemidemi-semiquaver** or **sixty-fourth note** ♪ is half as long as a demisemiquaver.

This diagram shows the relationship between the different note values.

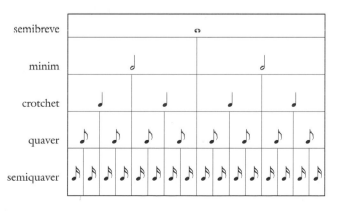

Notation and grouping of notes

Position of note-stems

When only one set of notes is written on a stave, you may see some notes (minims, crotchets, quavers and semiquavers) have a stem going up (♩), while others have a stem going down (♩). The value of each type of note is exactly the same, but the stems are written up (on the right-hand side) when the note is lower than the middle line of the stave, and down (on the left-hand side) when the note is above the middle line, like this:

If a note is on the middle line of the stave, you can choose whether the stem goes up or down. A good guide is to look at other notes nearby and follow the same pattern. Here are two examples:

The position of the stem does not affect the time value of the note, neither does the clef affect the position of the stem. A series of notes on the stave would normally look like this:

Here, the note-stem of B (on the middle line) may go up or down.

Exception to the rule

1 If we write two or more melodies on the same stave, the above rules do not always apply. Vocal music can be written like this:

soprano
alto

2 When notes such as quavers and semiquavers are joined, or beamed together, the stems of the notes in a group should all be written in the same direction, that is, either all upwards or all downwards. A group which contains notes written above and below the middle line is still beamed together in this way.

3 Keyboard music can be written like this:

Position of tails on notes

The tails, sometimes called **hooks** or **flags**, found on quavers and notes of lesser value are always placed on the right of the stem like this:

Grouping of notes

In instrumental music, and sometimes nowadays in vocal music, the stems of groups of quavers and notes of lesser value can be joined together to indicate each beat of the bar. So ♪♪ has the same value as ♫, and ♪♪♪♪ has the same value as ♫♫ Here is an example illustrating the correct grouping of notes:

Exception to the rule

In vocal music the syllables in the words can influence the grouping of the notes. You will often see notes that should be grouped together in instrumental music written, in vocal music, as separate notes:

Here is a ve-ry sim-ple lit-tle tune

Dotted notes

The note values that we have looked at so far have included the semibreve, minim, crotchet, quaver and semiquaver. If we want to write a note that is of a different time value from these, we could use a **dotted note.** If we place a dot after a note it makes the note half as long again, so that:

The curved line joining notes together is called a tie.

An important point to remember is that the dot must be placed **after** the note, like this: ♩.

A dot placed above or below a note like this ˙♩ does not increase its length. It is an instruction to play the note **staccato**, which means short and detached.

If we wish to join a dotted quaver ♪. and a semiquaver ♬ together, we can write it like this ♪♬ or this ⌐⌐

A quaver ♪ and two semiquavers ♬♬ are joined like this ♫♫ or this ⌐⌐

Double dot

A second dot or **double dot** adds a further one half of the value of the first dot. For example:

Rests

If we require an instrument or voice to be silent during a piece of music it is necessary to write a rest, or rests, to indicate this. For each note value, such as the semibreve, minim or crotchet, for example, there is an equivalent rest. Below is a table of rests:

breve		The breve rest fills the space between the 3rd and 4th lines. It is used to indicate a full bar's rest in $\frac{4}{2}$ time.
semibreve		The semibreve rest hangs below the 4th line. This rest can also be used for a full bar's rest in any time, although not generally used for this purpose in $\frac{4}{2}$ time.
minim		The minim rest sits on the 3rd line. It occurs in music where the beat is a minim, and in $\frac{4}{4}$, but never in $\frac{3}{4}$.
crotchet		The crotchet rest can be written in two ways, although 𝄽 is now used most frequently.
quaver		The quaver rest has one tail like the quaver note. ♪ It looks like the figure 7.
semiquaver		The semiquaver rest has two tails like the semiquaver note. ♬
demisemiquaver		The demisemiquaver rest has three tails like the demisemiquaver note. ♬

Dotted rests

Rests, like notes, can also be dotted. A dot placed after a rest makes the rest half as long again. Here are some examples:

Bar-lines

Examine the following tune. You will see that there are upright lines drawn through the stave at regular intervals.

Twinkle twinkle little star

These lines are called bar-lines. They divide the music into equal portions called **bars**, decided by the time signature (see below) and indicate the position of the first beat in the bar. A double bar-line ‖ indicates the end of the music, or the end of a section of the music.

Time signatures

At the beginning of a piece of music you should find two numbers arranged like this $\frac{3}{4}$. Here is an example:

The numbers are called a **time signature.** A time signature is always placed at the beginning of a composition, immediately after the key signature. If there is no key signature, the time signature is written immediately after the clef.

A time signature provides valuable information. The top figure indicates how many beats, or divisions, there are in a bar, while the lower figure tells what sort of notes the beats are. For example:

$\frac{3}{4}$ = 3 beats in a bar
= the beats are crotchets (or quarter notes)

So, $\frac{3}{4}$ means that there are three crotchet beats in a bar. It does not mean that every bar has to have the repeated rhythm of three crotchet notes in it, as the music would obviously become extremely repetitive, like this.

What it does mean, is that every bar of music should have the equivalent of three crotchet beats. So, for example, in $\frac{3}{4}$ time you could use any appropriate combination of note values or rests. For example:

- A time signature should not be written as a fraction. For example, write $\frac{3}{4}$ not $\frac{3}{4}$
- The time signature may change in a piece of music. For each change, a new time signature must be added at the beginning of the bar where the change takes place.

The top figure of a time signature

The top figure of a time signature may tell you how many beats there are in a bar, but there is a difference between a **simple time signature** and a **compound time signature**. In simple time, the top figure (such as 2, 3, 4, 5, 7, and so on) tells you the number of beats in a bar. For example, if the top figure is 2, then there are two beats in a bar.

In compound time, the top figure (6, 9 or 12), if divided by three, will give you the number of beats in a bar. For example, an upper figure of 9 in compound time tells you that there are three beats in a bar.

The lower figure of a time signature

The lower figure will be 2, 4, 8, 16 (or, more rarely, 1, 32 or 64) and is an indication of the type of beat. It tells what proportion of a semibreve is used for each division. Below is a chart to explain the meaning of the lower figure of a time signature.

Lower figure	Type of beat	Written	Alternative note name
1	semibreve	o	whole note
2	minim	♩	half note
4	crotchet	♩	quarter note
8	quaver	♪	eighth note
16	semiquaver	♫	sixteenth note
32	demisemiquaver	♬	thirty-second note

Simple and compound time signatures

Time signatures can be either simple or compound. A simple time signature, such as $\frac{4}{2}, \frac{4}{4}, \frac{4}{8}$, indicates that the beat, or each division of the bar, divides into **two** equal notes (or rests). For example, $\frac{4}{4}$ means that there are four crotchet beats in every bar and each crotchet beat may be divided into two quaver notes or rests. Like this:

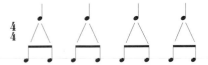

A compound time signature such as $\frac{6}{4}, \frac{6}{8}, \frac{6}{16}$, indicates that the beat divides into **three** equal notes (or rests). Each beat, or division of the bar, in compound time is equal to a dotted note. For example, $\frac{6}{8}$ means that there are two dotted crotchet beats in a bar, and each dotted crotchet beat may be divided into three quaver notes or rests. This makes a total of six quaver notes (or their equivalent) in a bar. Like this:

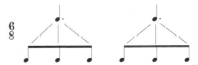

A simple time signature should not be confused with a compound time signature when both add up to the same total time value. For example, the simple time signature $\frac{3}{4}$ (three crotchets in a bar) and the compound time signature $\frac{6}{8}$ (six quavers in a bar) are **not** the same. The grouping of the notes and the rhythmic effect is quite different.

$\frac{3}{4}$ = ♩   ♩   ♩   (three crotchet beats)

$\frac{6}{8}$ = ♩.   ♩.   (two dotted crotchet beats)

The following tables illustrate simple and compound time signatures and the correct grouping of notes for each. Notice how each group of notes equals one beat.

A time signature is always placed at the beginning of the music after the clef and the key signature (if there is one). Remember the sequence clef, key signature, time signature (**c k t** in alphabetical order). Unless the time signature changes during a composition you will only need to write the time signature once at the beginning. The clef and key signature, however, should be written at the beginning of every stave:

SIMPLE TIME SIGNATURES			
SIMPLE DUPLE 2 beats in a bar	$\frac{2}{2}$ or ¢ ♩ ♩ ♩♩♩♩	$\frac{2}{4}$ ♩ ♩ ♫ ♫	$\frac{2}{8}$ ♪ ♪ ♬ ♬
SIMPLE TRIPLE 3 beats in a bar	$\frac{3}{2}$ ♩ ♩ ♩ ♩♩ ♩♩ ♩♩	$\frac{3}{4}$ ♩ ♩ ♩ ♫ ♫ ♫	$\frac{3}{8}$ ♪ ♪ ♪ ♬ ♬ ♬
SIMPLE QUADRUPLE 4 beats in a bar	$\frac{4}{2}$ ♩ ♩ ♩ ♩ ♩♩ ♩♩ ♩♩ ♩♩	$\frac{4}{4}$ ♩ ♩ ♩ ♩ ♫ ♫ ♫ ♫	$\frac{4}{8}$ ♪ ♪ ♪ ♪ ♬ ♬ ♬ ♬

Notice that instead of $\frac{4}{4}$ we can write c (common time), and instead of $\frac{2}{2}$ we can write ¢ (alla bre...

COMPOUND TIME SIGNATURES			
COMPOUND DUPLE 2 beats in a bar	$\frac{6}{4}$ ♩. ♩. ♩♩♩ ♩♩♩	$\frac{6}{8}$ ♩. ♩. ♫♫ ♫♫	$\frac{6}{16}$ ♪. ♪. ♬♬ ♬♬
COMPOUND TRIPLE 3 beats in a bar	$\frac{9}{4}$ ♩. ♩. ♩. ♩♩♩ ♩♩♩ ♩♩♩	$\frac{9}{8}$ ♩. ♩. ♩. ♫♫ ♫♫ ♫♫	$\frac{9}{16}$ ♪. ♪. ♪. ♬♬ ♬♬ ♬♬
COMPOUND QUADRUPLE 4 beats in a bar	$\frac{12}{4}$ ♩. ♩. ♩. ♩. ♩♩♩ ♩♩♩ ♩♩♩ ♩♩♩	$\frac{12}{8}$ ♩. ♩. ♩. ♩. ♫♫ ♫♫ ♫♫ ♫♫	$\frac{12}{16}$ ♪. ♪. ♪. ♪. ♬♬ ♬♬ ♬♬ ♬♬

Important points about rests and time signatures

1 Rests, like notes, must be grouped in a correct manner.
2 Apart from (a) the whole bar rest, and (b) the minim rest to denote a half bar's silence in $\frac{4}{4}$ time, shown below, **no rest longer than one beat should be used**.
   a A semibreve rest ▬ is used to indicate a whole bar's silence with any time signature, although it is generally not used in $\frac{4}{2}$ time
   b In $\frac{4}{4}$ time, one rest of two beats is written to denote a half bar's silence, but only at the beginning or end of a bar.

Notes of less than one beat have rests added to make up that beat, or subdivision of the beat, before other rests are added to complete the bar.

 is quite correct,

while this  is unsuitable.

Some examples to illustrate the correct grouping of rests:

(a)

(b)

Silence that can be indicated by a dotted rest can also be written with two rests of smaller value. Both of the following examples are correct:

In compound time, where there are three divisions of the beat, one rest is written to indicate silence for the first two of the three divisions of the beat.

while the last two divisions of the beat must have two rests.

Anacrusis

When a melody or phrase begins on a weak beat, it is called an **anacrusis**. If a composition begins with an incomplete bar, with one or more notes occurring before the first beat of the first complete bar, it is customary to make up the number of beats in the final bar, so that the first and last bars added together make one complete whole bar. For example, a melody beginning like this:

 should end with the equivalent of three crotchet beats, such as: etc.

Triplets and other irregular groups

Notes can be grouped together in irregular groups. The most frequently used group is the **triplet**. A triplet is a group of three notes, all of equal time value, played in the time of two. The figure 3 is written above or below the notes and a slur or bracket is usually added.

Triplet quavers are of equal value to two quavers.

Triplet crotchets are of equal value to two crotchets.

Triplets may include a rest or rests written, for example like this:

As a rule, if you wish to have an irregular group of notes, it is customary to write the number of notes above or below the group.

Examples of irregular groups

Duplet
A duplet is a group of two notes performed in the time of 3 of the same kind.

Quadruplet
A quadruplet is a group of four notes performed in the time of 3 or 6.

Quintuplet

A quintuplet is a group of five notes performed in the time of 4 or 6 of the same kind.

Sextuplet

A sextuplet is a group of six notes to be performed in the time of 4.

Septolet

A septolet is a group of seven notes to be performed in the time of 4 or 6.

Ledger lines

Sometimes we need to write music above or below the range of notes that are available on the stave. In order to do this we have to add **ledger lines** (or **leger lines**) to our music. Ledger lines are short lines drawn above or below the stave. They simply extend the stave and allow us to write music as high or low as necessary.

The following examples show how notes are written on ledger lines in the treble and bass clef, although, of course, ledger lines may be used with any clef. The same pattern of line – space – line – space, found on the stave, continues with ledger lines. The distance between each ledger line is the same as the distance between each line of the stave. There are notes even higher and lower than those illustrated below. Should you need to write them, just continue the pattern shown:

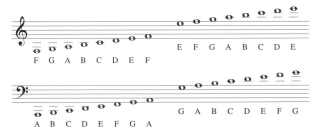

When it is necessary to write very high or very low notes which would require many ledger lines, the notes may be written one octave lower (or higher), and the sign **8** or **8va** (**ottava**) added. This indicates that the notes must be played one octave higher (or lower) than written. The sign, written over (or under) the first note of the ottava section, is followed by a continuous or dotted line above (or below)

the music for as long as required. When the line ends, like this ⌐ or ⌐, written pitch is resumed. Occasionally, the word **loco** is also added to cancel the ottava instruction.

Ties, slurs and phrase marks

You will often see curved lines written on printed music. These lines serve three distinct purposes.

Ties

A tie is a curved line ⌣ or ⌢ joining two or more adjacent notes **of the same pitch** together. Only the first note is struck or sounded and then sustained continuously for the total length of time indicated by the notes which the tie joins together. A tie often connects two notes separated by a bar-line, or produces a time value which cannot be indicated by a single note.

In the first example, the tied G notes last for three crotchet beats, and the tied A notes last for five crotchet beats. In the second example, the tied F sharp notes last for six and a half crotchet beats, and the tied E notes last for two and a half crotchet beats.

Slurs

A slur is indicated by a curved line drawn over or under two or more notes which are **not of the same pitch**. A slur suggests that the notes be played smoothly together. For example, the slur in music for bowed instruments indicates that notes are to be played with one stroke of the bow, while in vocal music the slur shows that the notes marked must be sung in one breath, or that two or more notes are to be sung to one syllable. Slurs are also found in music for brass, woodwind and keyboard instruments. Slurs and ties can be placed above or below the notes, but are always written on the opposite side to the stems.

A slur may also suggest to the performer that the final note of the slur is slightly shortened. For example,

may become this in performance:

Phrase mark

A **phrase mark** or **phrasing mark** is a curved line placed above or below groups of notes indicating the division of a melody into smaller sections or phrases. Each musical phrase or motive is a natural division of the melodic line. Below is an example of a melody illustrating the use of phrase marks.

Au clair de la lune

Performers frequently experiment with phrasing, sometimes preferring their own interpretation to the printed suggestion. Some editions of music deliberately omit phrase marks. These omissions, however, are not the result of carelessness. Phrase marks are often left out because the original manuscript did not contain them, or dubious additions have been made by later editors and it is difficult to know exactly what the composer originally required.

Scales

A scale is a succession of single notes moving upwards or downwards, arranged in a regular pattern. There are many different types of scales. The scales we shall look at first all contain eight notes. They are the **major** and **minor** scales, and are both called **diatonic scales**.

The major scale

Examine a keyboard. If you play the white notes C D E F G A B C you will have just played a major scale, namely the ascending scale of C major. If the scale is written upon the stave, it looks like this:

Writing a major scale

1 A scale can begin on any note (not just C), but it must contain eight notes and finish on the same letter as it started. A scale of E flat major, for example, begins on the note E flat, contains eight notes and ends on the next E flat.

2 When written on the stave, the notes of a scale move alternately line – space – line – space, etc. (or, of course, space – line – space – line etc.) Any two consecutive notes of a scale are never written on the same line or space.

3 The major scale always uses a set pattern of intervals between the notes. If each note of the scale of C major is numbered, the following pattern results:

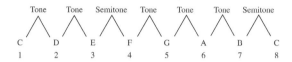

This pattern (T T S T T T S) now applies to every major scale.

Note: The scale of C major is the only scale without accidentals. Any other scale will contain one or more sharps, or one or more flats.

Writing the scale of D major

- To write the scale of D major, you may find it useful to refer to the keyboard:

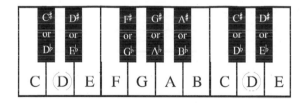

- Choose a suitable clef and decide whether to write the ascending (going up) or descending (going down) form of the scale. Here, we shall write the ascending scale of D major. Then, on the stave, write in notes number 1 and number 8. The scale of D major begins on a D and finishes on a D. The notes on this stave are semibreves, but other note values could be used.

- Add note number 2, using the pattern T T S T T T S. Look at the keyboard, and find the starting note D. Then find the note which is a tone above D. It is the note E.

- Add note number 3, a tone above E. That brings us to either F sharp or G flat. Remembering that a scale should move alternately line – space – line – space, etc, if we choose G flat it would definitely be the wrong note. We would move space – line – line. If we choose F sharp (definitely the correct note) we would move space – line – space.

(a) INCORRECT

(b) CORRECT

- Using the pattern TTSTTTS, work out the rest of the scale. Here is the ascending scale of D major.

ASCENDING

- The descending scale of D major looks like this:

DESCENDING

The semitones can be indicated by using slurs. In an ascending major scale semitones always occur between notes 3–4 and 7–8 (and descending 8–7 and 4–3).

Technical names

Instead of numbering the notes of a major or minor scale from 1 to 8, the technical names for each degree may be used. Each note of the scale has its own name as follows:

1 Tonic (or key note)
2 Supertonic
3 Mediant
4 Subdominant
5 Dominant
6 Submediant
7 Leading note
8 Tonic (or key note)

The scale of C major with each degree named, looks like this:

| TONIC | SUPERTONIC | MEDIANT | SUBDOMINANT | DOMINANT | SUBMEDIANT | LEADING NOTE | TONIC |

Scales with key signatures

In the examples given so far, we have written scales using **accidentals**, putting sharps or flats in front of the notes that needed them. Another way to write a scale is to use a **key signature** instead of accidentals. We still follow the rules for the construction of the scale (T T S T T T S), but instead of placing the accidentals in front of the notes, we put them at the beginning of the stave, following the clef.

Scale of D major with accidentals

Scale of D major with key signature

The key signature of D major tells us that all Fs and Cs are sharp. In the bass clef F sharp and C sharp are still required but are indicated in a different position on the stave.

Major key signatures

The sharps and flats of the major key signatures are written on the same lines and spaces as the notes to which they refer.

C major   G major   D major   A major   E major   B major   F♯ major   C♯ major

F major   B♭ major   E♭ major   A♭ major   D♭ major   G♭ major   C♭ major

Remembering key signatures

The following mnemonics will help you to remember the sequence of key signatures and the number of sharps or flats for each one:

Sharps

Good   Dogs   Always   Earn   Biscuits   F#or
1 sharp 2 sharps 3 sharps 4 sharps 5 sharps 6 sharps
C#runching
7 sharps

All the keys that have sharps in their key signature, with the exception of **F sharp major** (6 sharps) and **C sharp major** (7 sharps), do not use the word 'sharp' to identify the key. Thus, we say **G major, D major, A major, E major** and **B major**.

Flats

Flowers B♭loom E♭arly A♭nd   D♭on't G♭enerally
1 flat   2 flats   3 flats   4 flats   5 flats   6 flats
C♭omplain
7 flats

All the keys that have flats in their key signature, except **F major** (one flat), are identified by the word, 'flat'. Hence, we say **B flat major, E flat major, A flat major, D flat major, G flat major** and **C flat major.**

Order of sharps and flats

Sharps or flats in a key signature are **always** written in a particular order following this pattern:

Order of sharps

Order of flats

The minor scale

There are two types of minor scale, and each contains eight notes.

The harmonic minor scale

The ascending and descending scale of A harmonic minor is shown below:

Writing the harmonic minor scale

1 The harmonic minor scale can begin on any note, but it must contain eight notes and finish on the same letter as it started. The scale of **A harmonic minor**, for example, begins on the note A, contains eight notes and ends on the next A.

2 The harmonic minor scale (like the major scale) uses the same notes in both ascending and descending sequence. This is an important point as the other type of minor scale (the melodic minor) has a different sequence when descending.

3 When written on the stave, the notes of the scale move alternately line – space – line – space, etc. (or, of course, space – line – space – line etc.). Any two consecutive notes of a scale are never written on the same line or space.

4 The harmonic minor scale always uses a set pattern of intervals between the notes. The pattern of whole tones and semitones is different from the major scale. The sequence is:

5 The leap of one and a half tones or three semitones is called an **augmented 2nd** and gives this scale a distinctive character.

The melodic minor scale

The ascending and descending scale of A melodic minor is shown below:

Writing the melodic minor scale

1 The melodic minor scale can begin on any note, but it must contain eight notes and finish on the same letter as it started. The scale of A melodic minor, for example, begins on the note A, contains eight notes and ends on the next A.

2 The melodic minor scale does not have the same notes in the descending form as it does when it ascends. The sixth and seventh notes are each raised one semitone when ascending, and then restored when descending. This gives a smoother scale than the harmonic minor, avoiding the leap of an augmented 2nd (three semitones).

3 When written on the stave, the notes of the scale move alternately line – space – line – space, etc. (or, of course, space – line – space – line etc.). Any two consecutive notes of a scale are never written on the same line or space.

4 The pattern of tones and semitones is different from both the major scale and the harmonic minor scale. The melodic minor scale has the following sequence:

Ascending

Descending

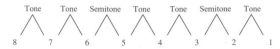

Minor key signatures

We can write a minor scale with a key signature and accidentals where required, or without a key signature but showing all the accidentals. When writing a minor scale with a key signature, both the harmonic form and the melodic form of the scale will share the same key signature. For example:

Ascending scale of C harmonic minor with key signature

Ascending scale of C melodic minor with key signature

Ascending scale of C harmonic minor without key signature

Ascending scale of C melodic minor without key signature

The following examples illustrate the ways in which an ascending and descending minor scale can be written.

G harmonic minor with key signature

G harmonic minor without key signature

G melodic minor with key signature

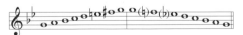

G melodic minor without key signature

For each major key, there is a corresponding minor key sharing the same key signature. This is called the **relative minor**. For each minor key, there is a corresponding major key sharing the same key signature, called the **relative major.** The tonic note (or key note) of the relative minor key is found one and a half tones (three semitones) lower

than the tonic note of the major key. Here are the scales of F major and D minor:

F major

D harmonic minor

F major and D minor share the same key signature. If you noticed the key signature of one flat at the beginning of the music you would not immediately be able to tell if the key was F major or D minor. The clue would be found in the actual music. D minor requires a C sharp which F major does not. Another clue may be found at the end of the music, by checking whether the last note is an F or a D. The following two examples illustrate the above point. Tune (a) is in the key of F major and Tune (b) is in the key of D minor.

Table of major and relative minor key signatures

C major A minor	G major E minor	D major B minor	A major F♯ minor
E major C♯ minor	B major G♯ minor	F♯ major D♯ minor	C♯ major A♯ minor
F major D minor	B♭ major G minor	E♭ major C minor	A♭ major F minor
D♭ major B♭ minor	G♭ major E♭ minor	C♭ major A♭ minor	

The chromatic scale

The chromatic scale contains 12 different notes, and consists entirely of semitones. On the keyboard, a chromatic scale can be found by starting on any note, and playing all the black and white notes, moving up or down through one octave.

Chromatic scales can be written in a number of ways (as shown below), although composers generally tend to use whichever form of chromatic scale produces fewest accidentals and is easiest to read.

The two forms of chromatic scale are the **harmonic chromatic scale** and the **melodic chromatic scale** (also referred to as the **arbitrary chromatic scale**).

The **harmonic chromatic scale** has the same form ascending and descending, and is the same whether in a major or a minor key. To write this scale (here we show the harmonic chromatic scale of C), first write each degree of the scale twice except the tonic (key-note) and the dominant, like this:

Then, add the correct accidental to produce a semitone between each note, like this:

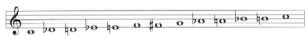

The **melodic chromatic scale**, when written in a major key, differs from that in a minor key. Additionally, melodic chromatic scales differ in their ascending and descending forms. To write the **ascending form of the melodic chromatic scale in a major key** (here we show the melodic chromatic scale of C major), first write each degree of the scale twice except the mediant and the leading note, like this:

Then, add the correct accidental to produce a semitone between each note, like this:

The **descending form of the melodic chromatic scale in a major key** is like that of the harmonic chromatic scale (with one tonic, one dominant and two notes on all the other degrees):

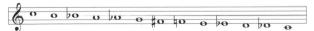

To write the **ascending form of the melodic chromatic scale in a minor key** (here we show the melodic chromatic scale of C minor), first write the notes of both the harmonic minor and melodic minor scales and then add the remaining chromatic semitones, like this:

The descending form of the melodic chromatic scale in a minor key is like that of the harmonic chromatic scale.

Double sharps and double flats

Sometimes it is necessary to raise or lower a note by **two semitones**. This requires a **double sharp** or a **double flat**. Like all accidentals, the sign for a double sharp or a double flat is always written on the same line or space as the note to which it refers.

- A double sharp raises a note two semitones and is written like this ×
- A double flat lowers a note two semitones and is shown by two flat signs ♭♭
- A double sharp or double flat can be made natural by writing two natural signs ♮♮ although it is now common practice to use just one natural sign ♮
- A double sharp can be brought back to one sharp (i.e. by one semitone) by writing a natural sign with a sharp sign: ♮♯
- A double flat can be brought back to one flat (i.e. by one semitone) by writing a natural sign with a flat sign: ♮♭

As with all accidentals, the double sharp or double flat affects the note before which it is placed, and any other subsequent notes placed on the same line or space throughout the bar.

If a note is tied into the next bar, any accidental affecting that note continues for the length of the tie.

C Clefs

The **C clef** is a moveable clef which is placed on the stave to indicate the position of middle C. C clefs can sometimes be found in vocal music, although they are rarely used now, and in music for some orchestral instruments. The viola normally uses a C clef. Other instruments, for example the bassoon, cello and tenor trombone, may use a C clef when the music is too high for the bass clef, in order to reduce the number of ledger lines. Normally, this clef is now used to indicate that either the third or fourth line of the stave is middle C.

Centred on the third line, the C clef is also known as the **alto clef**; centred on the fourth line, it is also known as the **tenor clef**.

The alto clef

The C clef centred on the third line of the stave is usually referred to as the alto clef. It is the normal clef for the viola and is written like this:

or this:

The third line is middle C. When using the alto clef, you may imagine the top two lines of the stave as belonging to the treble clef, and the lower two lines belonging to the bass clef.

middle C

Notes in the alto clef

C D E F G A B C D E F G A

The opening bars of Twinkle Twinkle Little Star beginning on middle C, and written in the alto clef.

Just as sharps or flats in a key signature always appear in a regular order in the treble and bass clefs, so also in the alto clef.

The tenor clef

The C clef centred on the fourth line up of the stave is usually referred to as the tenor clef. It is sometimes used in music written for bassoon, cello and tenor trombone when the music is too high for the bass clef. It is written like this:

or this:

The fourth line up is middle C. When using the tenor clef, you may imagine the top line of the stave as belonging to the treble clef, and the lower three lines belonging to the bass clef, like this:

middle C

Notes in the tenor clef

A B C D E F G A B C D E F

The opening bars of Twinkle Twinkle Little Star beginning on middle C, and written in the tenor clef.

The order of the sharps and flats in key signatures in the tenor clef is as follows:

Intervals: major, minor and perfect

An **interval** is the distance in pitch between two notes and is measured by counting the letter names from the lower note to the upper note. We can use the scale of C major to demonstrate how intervals are calculated and named.

1 2 3 4 5 6 7 8

For example, consider the interval between the note C and the note E. The interval can be written as a **harmonic interval** (the two notes occurring together) like this:

or as a **melodic interval** (the two notes occurring one after the other) like this:

Counting from the lower note we have C – D – E, three notes. Therefore this interval is a **3rd**. We always include the note we start on and the note we finish on. However, to call the interval just a 3rd is not accurate enough. We should also describe what kind of 3rd it is.

In the key of C major, the note C is called the **tonic note** or **key note**. All the other degrees of the scale of C major form intervals above the tonic note and are named like this:

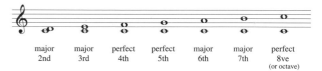

| major 2nd | major 3rd | perfect 4th | perfect 5th | major 6th | major 7th | perfect 8ve (or octave) |

The interval of C to E is called a **major 3rd**.

Some intervals that occur in a major key also appear in the minor key which has the same tonic note. These keys are referred to as the **tonic major** key and the **tonic minor** key. For example, look at the ascending and descending scale of C melodic minor with all the intervals named:

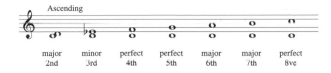

Ascending

major 2nd | minor 3rd | perfect 4th | perfect 5th | major 6th | major 7th | perfect 8ve

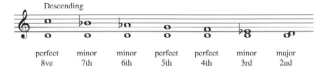

Descending

perfect 8ve | minor 7th | minor 6th | perfect 5th | perfect 4th | minor 3rd | major 2nd

The major 2nd (C – D), perfect 4th (C – F), perfect 5th (C – G) and perfect octave (C – C) are the same in both keys, C major and C minor.

In the ascending scale of C melodic minor, the sixth and seventh notes (A and B) are the same as the sixth and seventh notes in the scale of C major, and so they share the same interval names. C to A is a **major 6th** and C to B is a **major 7th**.

However, in the descending form of the scale of C melodic minor, the sixth and seventh notes (A♭ and B♭) are different. The interval between C and A♭ is called a **minor 6th**, and the interval between C and B♭ is called a **minor 7th.**

When the notes of an interval are those which occur in a major or minor scale, it is said to be a **diatonic** interval. Below are all the major, minor and perfect intervals found in the combined keys of C major and C minor:

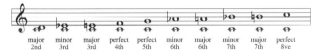

major 2nd | minor 3rd | major 3rd | perfect 4th | perfect 5th | minor 6th | major 6th | minor 7th | major 7th | perfect 8ve

The interval names shown above occur in all keys. For example, consider all the major, minor and perfect intervals found in the combined keys of E major and E minor. The tonic note is E:

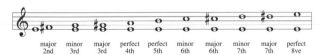

major 2nd | minor 3rd | major 3rd | perfect 4th | perfect 5th | minor 6th | major 6th | minor 7th | major 7th | perfect 8ve

Naming intervals

major 3rd | perfect 4th | perfect 5th | major 7th

Each of the above intervals is named by taking the lower note as the tonic note of a major or minor scale. However, the notes of an interval may also occur in several different keys, other than the particular major or minor key suggested by the lower note of the interval. Consider the perfect 5th (E – B) in the above example. The lower note (E) of the interval is taken to be the tonic note, suggesting the key of E major and/or E minor. Yet the notes of this interval, E and B can also be found in the key of C major,

D major, G major, A major, A minor, B major and B minor. While in these cases, the lower note (E) of the interval cannot be the tonic note, the interval remains a perfect 5th.

- When naming an interval, always take the lower note to be the tonic note and calculate the interval type and number from that note.
- The fact that an interval may also occur in a number of other keys does not affect the way that the interval is named.

More intervals: augmented and diminished

An interval one semitone more than perfect is augmented:

perfect 4th | augmented 4th | augmented 4th | perfect 5th | augmented 5th | augmented 5th

An interval one semitone less than perfect is diminished:

perfect 4th | diminished 4th | diminished 4th | perfect 5th | diminished 5th | diminished 5th

An interval one semitone more than major is augmented:

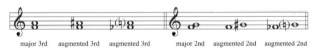

major 3rd | augmented 3rd | augmented 3rd | major 2nd | augmented 2nd | augmented 2nd

An interval one semitone less than major is minor:

major 3rd | minor 3rd | minor 3rd | major 2nd | minor 2nd | minor 2nd

An interval one semitone less than minor is diminished.

minor 3rd | diminished 3rd | diminished 3rd | minor 6th | diminished 6th | diminished 6th

Major and minor intervals may be changed as follows:

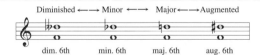

Diminished ⟷ Minor ⟶ Major ⟷ Augmented

dim. 6th | min. 6th | maj. 6th | aug. 6th

Perfect intervals may be changed as follows:

Diminished ⟷ Perfect ⟷ Augmented

dim. 5 | perf. 5 | aug. 5

Augmented and diminished intervals occur more frequently in minor scales.

Compound intervals

A compound interval is one which is greater than an octave. For example:

A compound major 2nd is the same as a major 9th

A compound major 3rd is the same as a major 10th

A compound minor 3rd is the same as minor 10th

The magic seven

For intervals greater than an octave, deduct seven from the interval number to check its type. For example:
- A major 9th is the same as a compound major 2nd $(9 - 7 = 2)$.
- A major 10th is the same as a compound major 3rd $(10 - 7 = 3)$.
- A minor 10th is the same as a compound minor 3rd $(10 - 7 = 3)$.

Inversions of intervals

When an interval is **inverted** it is turned upside down. Either the lower note is taken up an octave leaving the upper note unmoved, or the higher note is taken down an octave leaving the lower note unmoved. The inverted interval, A to F, in this example, becomes exactly the same interval using either method. Only the position on the stave is changed.

The magic nine

When the numbers of the two intervals before and after inversion are added together, the answer will always be 9. For example:

A major 3rd becomes a minor 6th (3 + 6 = 9)

A perfect 4th becomes a perfect 5th (4 + 5 = 9)

Inversion numbers
The inversion of a 2nd is a 7th
The inversion of a 3rd is a 6th
The inversion of a 4th is a 5th
The inversion of a 5th is a 4th
The inversion of a 6th is a 3rd
The inversion of a 7th is a 2nd

Inversion names		
Perfect	– becomes –	Perfect
Minor	– becomes –	Major
Major	– becomes –	Minor
Diminished	– becomes –	Augmented
Augmented	– becomes –	Diminished

Some intervals and their inversions

Transposition

The two versions of the opening bars of the well-known tune *Old MacDonald had a Farm*, are different. All the notes in version **b** have been moved up a tone. This process is called **transposition**. Transposition is defined as the writing or performance of music at a different pitch from its original. The pitch of the notes is changed, and each note is moved exactly the same distance, but without making any other change to the music.

Music can be transposed by what ever interval is necessary to suit a particular high or low voice, or to put it in a suitable key for a particular instrument. In the example *Old MacDonald had a Farm*, each note was moved up a tone (the interval of a major 2nd), and the melody transposed from one key (C major) to a new key (D major).

Old MacDonald had a Farm

The easiest transpositions are those up or down one octave as the same letter names are always used. Here are some examples of the first four bars of *Twinkle Twinkle Little Star* transposed up and down by one or more octaves.

(a) Original

(b) Up one octave

Up two octaves
(c)

(d) Down one octave

(e) Down two octaves

If you are not sure where the notes an octave above or below a given note are to be found on the stave, this diagram should help you:

Look, for example, at middle C. Find the C one octave higher, and then the C two octaves higher than middle C. Now move down from middle C and find the C one octave lower in the bass clef, and so on.

Some instruments are called **transposing instruments**. When they play from the written music the result actually sounds at a different pitch. For example, the piccolo sounds one octave higher than written, and the double bass sounds one octave lower than written. The B♭ clarinet sounds one tone (a major 2nd) lower than written, and the F horn sounds a perfect 5th lower than written. Instruments transpose for the convenience of the performer and for practical reasons. For example, it can minimise the number of ledger lines required on the written part, or allow the performer to use the same fingering techniques for instruments of different sizes. More information about transposing instruments can be found in Chapter 24, 25 and 26.

Below are some examples to illustrate transposition using intervals other than an octave. The opening bars of the British National Anthem in G major have been transposed into several new keys.

Original in the key of G major

Transposed up a major 2nd to
the key of A major

Transposed up a minor 3rd to the
key of B♭ major

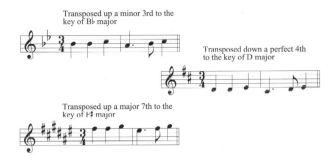

Transposed down a perfect 4th
to the key of D major

Transposed up a major 7th to the
key of F♯ major

Fortunately, transposition can always be double-checked to ensure that the exercise is completed accurately. The two methods are to transpose by **interval** (each note is transposed the required interval), and then to check each note in relation to its **key**. Look at the opening of *What shall we do with the drunken sailor*:

Let us suppose we have to transpose this sea shanty from the key of D minor up a minor third. One method is to **transpose each melody note by the required interval**. Firstly, decide upon the new key. The interval of a minor 3rd above D is F. Therefore, we move from D minor to F minor. (A tune in a minor key when transposed will always move to another minor key; never transpose a minor key into a major key. Similarly, a tune in a major key when transposed will always move to another major key.) Having established the new key, write the new key signature and move each note of the melody up the interval of a minor 3rd. The first note A moves up a minor 3rd to C, and so on.

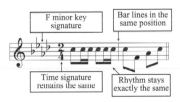

Now go through the whole transposition again, using a different method to check your working. This time, **consider each melody note and its position in relation to both the original and the new key**. The thinking process would be:

1 The original key of the melody is D minor.
2 The first note of the melody in the original key is A.
3 A is the 5th degree (dominant) of the scale of D minor.
4 Whatever key we move to we must write the first note as the 5th degree (dominant) of the scale in the new key.
5 We are moving to F minor and the 5th degree of the scale of F minor is the note C.
6 Double check to see if we decided that C was the first note using the **interval method**.

7 We did!

8 Now check all the remaining notes in this way.

Using the **key method** of transposition, any accidentals that appear can no longer cause problems. If the original melody looked like this

with notes 4, 5 and 6 changed, the thinking process would be:

1 The original key of the melody is D minor.

2 In the key of D minor, note 1 (A) is the 5th degree (dominant) of the scale.

3 Therefore, in the new key of F minor, note 1 must also be the 5th degree (dominant) of the scale. The new note is C.

4 We can also now add notes 2 and 3 as they are the same pitch.

5 In the key of D minor, note 4 (A flat) is the 5th degree of the scale lowered one semitone.

6 Therefore, in the new key of F minor, note 4 must also be the 5th degree of the scale lowered by one semitone. The new note is C flat.

7 Notes 5 and 6 can also be added, as they are the same pitch.

8 Note 7 (A), like notes 1, 2 and 3, is the 5th degree of the scale, and must be the note C in the new key, and so on.

The transposed melody looks like this:

The main point to remember when transposing accidentals is always to say that the note is **raised** or **lowered** by a semitone, or a tone. Never say that a note is sharpened or flattened. This could lead to inaccuracies. For example:

Theme	Transposed up a major 2nd	Transposed up a minor 3rd
Key: D minor	Key: E minor	Key: F minor

The accidental in example C has become a natural, while the accidental in examples (a) and (b) must be written as a sharp.

As a final check to ensure that you have correctly transposed the melody, play the original music and the transposition. They should sound exactly the same, except that each is in a different key.

Transpositions do not always have to be written out. Transposing can also be practised as a practical skill. This means that you transpose music at sight (however slowly at first), either singing or playing on an instrument. While you look at the music in the original key, you sing or play the notes in the new key. It is not as difficult as it sounds, and it is a valuable skill to develop.

Terms and signs

A list of terms and signs which are commonly found in music, follows. Many of them are of Italian origin and some are used less frequently than others. Use this part of the book as a reference section when studying or performing the music of other composers, or when you require information about terms and signs for your own compositions.

Speed

grave: very slow, solemn

lento: very slow

largo: broad, slow

larghetto: rather slow, but not as slow as largo

adagio: slow, leisurely

adagietto: rather slow

andante: at a walking pace, moderate speed

andantino: slower than andante; also faster than andante (andantino is an ambiguous term.)

moderato: moderate speed

allegretto: fairly quick, but not as quick as allegro

allegro: quick, merry, lively

vivace: vivacious, lively, quick

presto: very fast

prestissimo: as fast as possible

presto possibile: as fast as possible

tempo comodo: convenient or easy speed

tempo giusto: in strict time

- Words can be combined to give additional meaning about speed or style. For example: *Allegro ma non troppo, Allegro vivace e con brio, Allegro deciso*

Changes of speed

accelerando (**accel.**): accelerating, gradually getting faster

ad libitum (**ad lib.**): to be performed as the performer wishes or that an instrument or voice may be omitted

allargando: broader, becoming slower

a piacere: to be performed as the performer wishes

a tempo: return to the original speed following a speed change such as rall. or accel.

doppio movimento: twice as fast, double the speed

incalzando: getting quicker, more intense

l'istesso tempo: at the same speed

meno mosso: slower

piu mosso: quicker

rallentando (**rall.**): gradually slower

ritardando (**ritard., rit.**): gradually slower

ritenuto (**riten., rit.**): held back

stringendo: gradually faster

Intensity of sound

molto pianissimo (**ppp**): as quiet as possible

pianissimo (**pp**): very quiet

piano (**p**): quiet

mezzo piano (**mp**): moderately quiet

mezzo forte (mf): moderately loud

forte (f): loud

fortissimo (ff): very loud

molto fortissimo (fff): as loud as possible

calando: dying away, becoming quieter

morendo: dying away

perdendosi: dying away

smorzando: dying away

forzato, forzando (fz): accented, forcing the tone, suddenly loud

rinforzato, rinforzando (rf, rfz, rinf.): accented, forcing the tone, suddenly loud

sforzato, sforzando (sf, sfz): accented, forcing the tone, suddenly loud

crescendo (cresc., cres.) or ————————— : gradually louder

decrescendo (decresc., decres.) or ————————— : gradually quieter

diminuendo (dim.): gradually quieter

Expression and style

a cappella: in the church style, often means unaccompanied choral singing

à deux, à 2, a due, a 2: direction in orchestral or band music indicating that two instruments notated on one stave are to play in unison.

affettuoso: affectionately

affrettando: hurrying

agitato: agitated

alla marcia: in the style of a march

animato: animated, lively

appassionato: impassioned

arco: the bow of a string instrument (instruction to resume using the bow following pizzicato)

assai: very much

attacca: go on at once (to the next movement or section of the music)

ben: well

ben marcato: well marked, accented

bis: twice

bravura: with boldness and brilliance

brillante: brilliant

brio: vigour; spirit

cantabile: in a singing style

col, colla or **colle**: with, with the

comodo: easily, not hurrying

con: with

con anima: with feeling or with spirit

con brio: with vigour

con espressione: with expression

con forza: with force

con fuoco: with fire

con moto: with movement

con sordino: with mute

con spirito: with spirit

da capo (D.C.): from the beginning

dal segno (D.S.): from the sign (the sign is written 𝄋 or :𝄋:)

deciso: with firmness, boldly

delicato: delicate

divisi (div.): divided; often refers to string players in the orchestra dividing into two or more groups

dolce: sweetly

dolente: sadly

doloroso: grieving, sorrowfully

doppio movimento: twice as fast

doucement: sweetly, quietly

e: and

energico: with energy

espressione: expression

espressivo, espress., espr.: expressively

fin, fine: end

forza: force, emphasis

fuoco: fire

furioso: furiously

giocoso: gaily, playful

giusto: strict, exact

grandioso: grandly

grazioso: gracefully

impetuoso: impetuous

lacrimoso: weeping, sad

langsam: slow

largamente: broadly

legatissimo: as smoothly as possible

legato: smooth

leggiero: light

lento: slow

l'istesso: the same

loco: resume normal pitch (cancels 8va sign)

lusingando: coaxing, soothingly

ma: but

ma non troppo: but not too much

maestoso: majestic, stately

main droit (M.D., m.d.): right hand

mano destra (M.D., m.d.): right hand

main gauche (M.G., m.g.): left hand

mano sinistra (M.S., m.s.): left hand

marcato: marked, accented

martelé, martellato: hammered, strongly accented (manner of bowing stringed instruments; also a technique of piano playing)

meno: less

mesto: sad

misterioso: mysterious

molto: much

mosso: with movement, animated

nobilmente: nobly

non: not

non troppo: not too much

ossia: or, otherwise

ottava: octave

pastorale: in pastoral style

pesante: heavy

piacevole: pleasantly

piangevole: plaintively

più: more

pizzicato (pizz.): pluck the string

poco: a little

poco a poco: little by little

pomposo: pompous

prima, primo: first

quasi: as if, like, in the style of

rapido: rapid

rigoroso: strictly

risoluto: resolute, bold

ritmico: rhythmically

rubato (tempo rubato): 'robbed' time: to be performed with some freedom as to time, giving the music expression

scherzando: joking, playful

secondo: second, second time, second part

segue: follow on, continue

semplice: simple

sempre: always

senza: without

serioso: seriously

simile: continue in a similar manner

sostenuto: sustained

staccato (stacc.): short and detached

staccatissimo: very detached

strepitoso: noisy, boisterous

subito (sub.): suddenly

sul, sulla: on the

sul G: on the G string

sul ponticello: play near the bridge

tacet: it is silent; instruction that an instrument or voice is not required for a whole movement or section of the music.

tanto: so much

tempo: speed

tenuto: held

tranquillo: tranquil, calm

trionfale: triumphant

troppo: too much

tutti: all, the entire ensemble

veloce: swift, quick

vif: lively

vigoroso: vigorous

vite: quick

vivo: lively

volante: in a light, flying manner

volti subito (V.S.): turn over the page immediately

Abbreviations and signs

D.C. **da capo**: repeat from the beginning

D.S. **dal segno**: repeat from the sign (𝄋 or :𝄋:)

ppp **molto pianissimo**: as quietly as possible

pp **pianissimo**: very quiet

p **piano**: quiet

mp **mezzo piano**: moderately quiet

mf **mezzo forte**: moderately loud

f **forte**: loud

ff **fortissimo**: very loud

fff **molto fortissimo**: as loud as possible

fz **(forzato, forzando)** ⎫ accented, forcing

rf, rfz, rinf., **(rinforzato, rinforzando)** ⎬ the tone,

sf, sfz **(sforzato, sforzando)**: ⎭ suddenly loud

> ∧ ∨ accent the note

staccato, stacc.: ♩ ♩̇ short and detached

◁▷ **cresc., cres. (crescendo)**: gradually louder

▷◁ **decresc., decres. (decrescendo)**: gradually quieter

dim., dimin. (diminuendo): gradually quieter

M.D., m.d. (main droit, mano destra): right hand

M.G., m.g. (main gauche): left hand

M.S., m.s. (mano sinistra): left hand

M.M.: Maelzel's metronome; a mechanical (or electronic) device for sounding the exact number of beats required per minute.

M.M. ♩ = 60: This is a metronome mark meaning sixty crotchet beats a minute.

𝄢 : pedal; depress the piano damper pedal.

con ped., col ped.: with the pedal

pizz. (pizzicato): pluck the string

con sord. (con sordino): with the mute

div. (divisi): divided, often refers to string players in the orchestra dividing into two or more groups

rall. (rallentando): gradually slower

rit., ritard. (ritardando): gradually slower

rit., riten. (ritenuto): held back, slower at once

sim. (simile): continue in a similar manner

V.S. (volti subito): turn over the page immediately

⌢ A pause sign (or *fermata*) written above or below a note or rest prolongs it as long as the performer wishes. The instruction **G.P.** (general pause) is used in orchestral music to signify a rest for all the performers.

A curved line written above or below the notes will be a **tie**, **slur** or **phrase mark**. Their use is explained fully on pages 174 and 175.

Accents are indicated in a number of ways. For example:

Staccato: a dot over or under a note indicates that it is to be performed in a short, detached manner.

A **break** in the music can be indicated by two short lines // and a slight break by a comma ,

8va **signs** (see also page 174) indicate that the notes must be played one octave higher or lower than written. The sign 8va or **8** is followed by a continuous or dotted line above (or below) the music. Sometimes the word **loco** is added to indicate a return to the written pitch.

8va **bassa**, or 8va **sotto** may also be written under the notes of the bass stave to indicate that they are to be played one octave lower.

In an **arpeggio** the notes of a chord are played quickly, one after another beginning with the lowest note and sustaining the whole chord in 'harp' fashion.

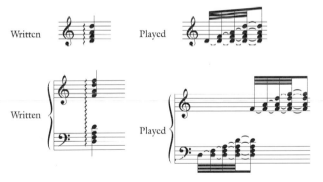

The arpeggio may be sounded downwards from the highest note which is indicated with this sign ⌡ or this sign ⌡⌡

Abbreviations of notation

To save time and space, and make the music easier to read, it is possible to use musical abbreviations. Some of the more commonly used abbreviations are shown below.

Reiterated notes are two or more notes of the same pitch and same time value which repeat immediately after each other. Instead of writing them out fully, they may be written as a single note with one or more strokes written above or below it (if the note is a semibreve) or through its stem. One stroke represents quavers, two strokes semiquavers and three strokes, demi-semiquavers. The notes to be played must be equal in value to the written abbreviated note.

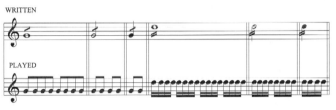

Rapid alternation of two or more notes may be written like this:

Notes to be reiterated or alternated as quickly as possible may be indicated with the word **tremolando**, **tremolo**, or **trem**.

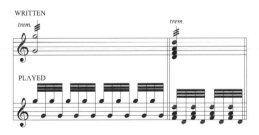

Repeated groups of notes are shown like this:

Repeated bars are shown like this:

This sign (𝄍) is rarely used in music for piano, organ and keyboard instruments.

Rests for any number of bars (more than one) may be written in several different ways. Some examples are shown below:

A **repeated section** or **movement** may be indicated by a double bar-line preceded by two or four dots. The music is repeated from the previous double bar-line with dots to the right of it. If the passage to be repeated is at the beginning of the music, as in example (c), the first set of dots are not usually written.

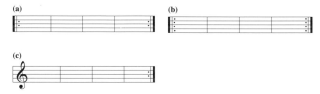

First and **second time bars** indicate that the music must be played to the end of the first time bar and then repeated from the beginning, or from the previous double bar-line with repeat dots to the right of it. On the repeat of the music, the first-time bar is omitted, and the second-time bar played instead.

Ornaments

The most commonly used ornaments are: the **trill** (or **shake**), the **mordent**, the **turn,** the **appoggiatura** and the **acciaccatura**. There are many variations in the writing and performing of ornaments. The following examples serve only as guidelines and generalisations to correct practice.

The trill or shake (*tr* or *tr*〜〜〜)

The **trill** is a rapid alternation of the given note and the note above it, written in demi-semiquavers. The trill in modern music usually begins on the written (or principal) note, while in music written up to the early nineteenth century, the trill generally begins on the note above the written note. The trill always ends on the written note.

Unless the trill is to be a very short one, this ornament frequently ends with a turn (see page 189), although you will find examples where a turn is not included. It will, nevertheless, still end on the written note.

Trill or shake beginning on the written note

Any trill, may end with a turn, and if this is to be included in a trill that begins on the written note, it will be necessary to show a triplet in the trill, as in examples a, b and c. This will ensure that the turn will end on the principal note and still 'add up' to the correct time value. Some composers will add two small notes (examples c and d) to indicate that the trill must end with a turn.

If a turn is included in a trill which begins on the note above the principal note, it will not be necessary to include a triplet (example f).

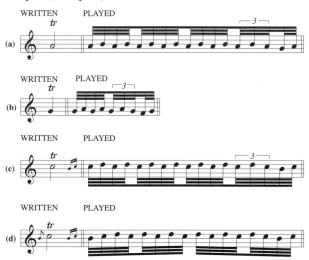

Trill beginning on the note above the written note

A trill will begin on the note above the principal note only when:

- an acciaccatura is written before the principal note to indicate this (examples e and f).
- the note before the principal note of the trill is the same note as the principal note (example g).
- the music belongs to an earlier period, up to and including the music of Haydn and Mozart.

If you want to write a trill that begins on the note above or below the principal note, it is now customary to indicate this with an acciaccatura. Examples e and f illustrate two different, but correct ways to play this trill.

The mordent

The **mordent** or **upper mordent** (~) is a shake of a very short duration. It consists of three notes: the written note, the note above, and the written note.

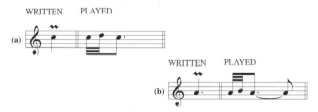

An **inverted mordent** or **lower mordent** (~) consists of the written note, the note below and the written note.

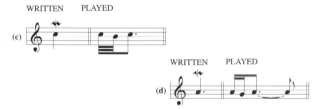

An accidental above a mordent refers to the upper note. An accidental below a mordant refers to the lower note.

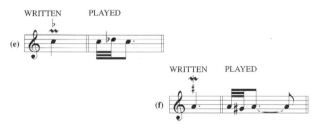

If the note is longer than a crotchet, such as in examples b, d and f, treat it as a crotchet and then tie on the remaining value as required.

The turn

The **turn** (or **grupetto**) usually consists of four notes:
- the note above the written note
- the written note
- the note below
- the written note

There are different ways to interpret the turn, depending on the speed and the character of the music. As with other ornaments, in performance, much is left to the performer's discretion.

If the sign ∾ is written over a note, the turn can be played like this:

If the sign ∾ is written between two notes, the turn can be played like this:

When the sign is written after a dotted note, the last note of the turn receives the value of the dot:

An accidental written above or below the sign indicates which note or notes require an accidental:

An **inverted turn**, indicated by either ∾ or ∾ , begins on the note below the written note:

The appoggiatura

The **appoggiatura** (a 'leaning' note) is a small note placed before the principal note and usually receives half the time value of the note which follows it.

When written before a dotted note, the appoggiatura takes two-thirds of that note.

Notice how the small-size notes, or **grace notes**, in the above examples, do not affect the written time value of the large-size note or notes in those bars where the grace notes appear. The large-size note(s) in each bar makes up the correct number of beats, and the grace note has no effect on this.

The acciaccatura

The acciaccatura (a 'crushed' note) is a small-size note written like a quaver with a stroke through it, and is played as quickly as possible.

23
Vocal ranges

Voices are usually divided into four groups: soprano, alto, tenor and bass. The vocal ranges given here are approximate. Trained singers may be able to exceed these limits.

Soprano

The highest type of female voice.

The soprano range is also the vocal range of a **treble**, a boy with an unbroken voice.

Alto and contralto

Alto: very high type of male voice.
Contralto: the lowest type of female voice.

The alto part can be sung by an alto or a contralto. Each has the same range, slightly lower than a soprano. A female with this vocal range is called a **contralto**, although a group of contraltos may also be referred to as altos. A male with this vocal range is called an **alto**.

In oratorio, opera, light opera and musicals, the alto chorus part is usually intended for women's voices. The alto part sung by men's voices is most frequent in cathedral and church choirs. The male alto uses the vocal technique called **falsetto**.

It is important to recognise that although a male voice and a female voice may have the same range, the quality of the voices will be different.

Tenor

The higher type of male voice.

Music for tenor voice can be written using either the bass clef or treble clef. In the bass clef, the music is written at its actual pitch, but when the treble clef is used, the music is sung one octave lower than written.

The tenor part using the bass clef is found in music for four-part choir which has been written on two, rather than four, staves. In this case, the tenor part shares a stave with

the bass part and both use the same bass clef. To distinguish the two parts, the tenor note stems always go upwards, and the bass note stems always go downwards. In the following example for four-part choir, the tenor and bass share the lower stave with a bass clef, while the soprano (note stems upwards) and alto (notes stems downwards) share the upper stave with a treble clef.

When each voice has its own stave, the tenor part is written in the treble clef, although it is sung one octave lower. The tenor part in the next example sounds at the same pitch as the tenor part in the previous example.

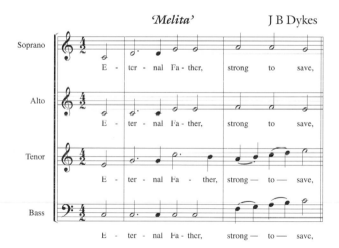

Sometimes, a small number 8 is written below the treble clef to indicate that the written notes are to be sung one octave lower:

Two treble clefs written together also indicate that the notes are to be sung one octave lower, although this sign is not frequently used.

Bass

The lowest type of male voice.

Other voices

Coloratura soprano: female voice, a soprano with great
  vocal agility and a very high range.
Mezzo-soprano: female voice, half-way between soprano
  and contralto range.
Counter-tenor: male voice, very high range, the same as
  an alto.
Baritone: male voice, half-way between tenor and bass
  range.
Basso profondo (**'deep bass'**): male voice, powerful and
  very low in range.

24
Stringed instruments

Stringed instruments are found in the orchestra, the string orchestra, and in ensembles such as the string quartet. They also feature as solo instruments.

Orchestral strings

The stringed instruments in the orchestra include the **violin, viola, cello** (abbreviated from **violoncello**, and sometimes written 'cello) and **double bass**. Each instrument has four strings, although some double basses have five strings. All these instruments can be bowed or plucked with the fingers.

When a string is pressed against the fingerboard of the instrument, it is called **stopping**. Often, these instruments play a single musical line, one note at a time, but it is possible for them to play chords of two, three and even four notes. The terms **double-stopping**, **triple-stopping** and **quadruple-stopping**, refer to the number of strings to be played at the same time. There are limitations to the combinations of notes that can be sounded together, and some combinations are more difficult to perform than others.

Bowing instructions and performance details

Bowing marks are indicated where necessary by these signs:

down bow   up bow

A **slur** is used to show if two or more notes are to be played with a single down or up stroke of the bow. This is an example of music for violin with bowing marks added:

Note: You do not have to put a bowing mark on every note. Only use bowing marks where you need them.

The Italian word **pizzicato**, or its abbreviation, **pizz.**, means pluck the note or notes. To resume bowing, the instruction **arco** (play with the bow) is used. A bowed **tremolo** is performed by rapidly repeating a single note with alternating down and up bow strokes. The tremolo is indicated by a number of slanting strokes drawn through the stem of the note if it has one, or placed above the note if it has not. Three strokes are used for a semibreve, minim and crotchet. Two strokes are used for a quaver, and one for a semiquaver, like this:

In very slow tempi, the abbreviation **trem.** may be added above the stave to indicate clearly that a tremolo is required. The instruction **con sordino**, (plural: con sordini) or the abbreviation **con sord.**, indicates that the mute is to be used, while **senza sord.** means take the mute(s) off. **Sul ponticello** is a direction to play with the bow as near to the bridge as possible, and **sul tasto** directs the player to bow near or above the fingerboard.

In the following section, the range of notes obtainable on the violin, viola, cello and double bass is given. It is important, however, to remember that the upper limits of these instruments will depend upon the skill of the performer, and that notes higher than the given upper limit are possible.

Violin

You may see music written for **first** and **second** violins. This does not mean that there are two different types of violins, nor that the first violins are better than the second violins. It simply means that the music for the violins will require two performers, or groups of performers, as the music will have two separate parts for the violins.

Orchestral stringed instruments may further divide into two or more smaller groups following the written instruction **divisi** or **div.**, showing that additional parts had been written for them.

Viola

Music for the viola is normally written using the C clef where middle C is on the third line (the alto clef). For the upper register, the viola can play in the treble clef to avoid the use of too many ledger lines.

Cello (violoncello)

Music for the cello is usually written in the bass clef. The tenor clef and the treble clef are also used for its higher, or highest, notes.

Open strings C G D A

Double bass

Music for the double bass is normally written in the bass clef. Although used quite rarely, the tenor clef and the treble clef may also be used for its higher and highest notes. The double bass always sounds one octave lower than written.

Open strings E A D G

Sounds one octave lower   Sounds one octave lower

Harp

The harp is also a member of the string family of the orchestra. Music for harp is written as for piano, on two bracketed staves, using the treble and bass clefs. Particularly effective on the harp are **arpeggios** and chords with up to four notes for either hand. The **glissando**, a scale played rapidly by sliding or sweeping the fingers across the strings is also often featured in music for harp.

Other stringed instruments

Guitar

The classical guitar and the electric guitar have six strings. Guitar music is written in the treble clef, one octave higher than it sounds. Notes higher than the upper extreme given here are possible.

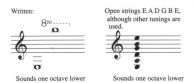

Written:

Open strings E A D G B E, although other tunings are used.

Sounds one octave lower   Sounds one octave lower

Electric bass guitar

The electric bass guitar has four, or sometimes five strings. The four-string electric bass is the more widely used of the two. Music for the electric bass guitar is written in the bass clef, but sounds one octave lower than written. Notes higher than the upper extreme given here are possible.

Open strings E A D G

Sounds one octave lower   Sounds one octave lower

25
Woodwind instruments

Woodwind instruments are found in the orchestra, concert wind band and the military band, and in numerous types of ensembles. They also feature as solo instruments. Woodwind instruments produce their sound in one of two ways. Sounds on the piccolo and flute are produced by blowing across a mouth-hole (the **embouchure**), while on the recorder, air is channelled against the edge of the sound-hole, through a whistle-mouthpiece. In both cases, the sounds produced are called **edge tones.** The instruments which produce these sounds are known as **flue instruments**. Alternatively, some woodwind instruments produce their sound by using a single or double cane reed.

Woodwind instruments can be classified as follows:
Flue instruments: recorders, piccolos and flutes
Single reed instruments: clarinets and saxophones
Double reed instruments: oboe, cor anglais, bassoon and double bassoon

Some members of the woodwind family are transposing instruments. They are identified below. Although generally the instrumental ranges given are extremes, additional notes exceeding the given ranges may be possible on some instruments by accomplished performers.

Recorder

Although once members of the orchestra, recorders are not found today in the modern orchestra. The five sizes of recorder are **sopranino**, **descant** (or **soprano**), **treble** (or **alto**), **tenor** and **bass**.

The compass of each instrument is:

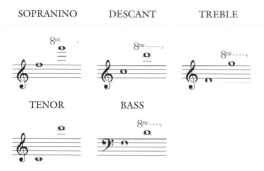

Music for the sopranino, descant and bass recorder is usually written one octave lower than it sounds. Occasionally, a small number 8 is added above the clef to indicate this:

Piccolo

The piccolo is a small flute. The **C piccolo** is more widely used than the **D-flat piccolo**, which is more common in the military band. To avoid the use of many ledger lines, music for piccolo is written one octave lower than it sounds. The written range of the C piccolo is:

but sounds:

Flute

The flute has a range of three octaves from middle C upwards. Some flutes, however, can exceed this range, producing the note B below middle C and the note D above the uppermost note given here:

Alto flute

The alto flute is a larger flute, sometimes referred to as the **G flute** or, somewhat inaccurately, as the **bass flute**. Although the written compass of the flute and the alto flute is the same, the alto flute is a transposing instrument and sounds a perfect 4th lower than written.

Clarinet

The clarinet is a transposing instrument. Most frequently found are the **B flat clarinet** and the **A clarinet**, although the B flat instrument is the more commonly used of the two. Other members of the clarinet family include the high **E flat clarinet** and the **B flat bass clarinet**. The **B flat contrabass clarinet** (sometimes called the **double-bass clarinet** or **pedal clarinet**) is rarely used.

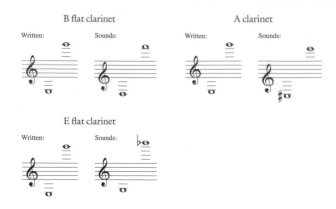

The B flat clarinet sounds a major 2nd lower than written, the A clarinet sounds a minor 3rd lower than written, and the E flat clarinet sounds a minor 3rd higher than written. The B flat bass clarinet has a range one octave lower than the B flat clarinet plus an additional semitone. Music for B flat bass clarinet may be written either in the bass clef (extending to the treble clef only for the higher notes), sounding a major 2nd lower than written. Or, as in much band music, it may be written entirely in the treble clef, sounding a major 9th lower than written.

B flat bass clarinet

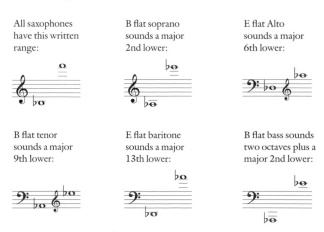

The B flat contrabass clarinet is pitched one octave below the B flat bass clarinet.

Saxophone

Saxophones have metal bodies but are played with a reed and are classed as woodwind instruments. Of the many sizes of saxophones that have been produced, the following five are the most frequently found: **B flat soprano, E flat alto, B flat tenor, E flat baritone** and **B flat bass**. All are transposing instruments and are written in the treble clef.

Oboe

The oboe is a non-transposing instrument. Music for the oboe sounds at the written pitch.

Cor anglais

The cor anglais (which in French means 'English horn') is really an alto oboe. It is a transposing instrument. Music for cor anglais sounds a perfect 5th lower than written.

Bassoon

The bassoon is a non-transposing instrument. The bassoon uses the bass clef and the tenor clef.

Double bassoon

The double bassoon is a transposing instrument, sounding one octave lower than written.

26
Brass instruments

Brass instruments are found in the orchestra, brass band, concert wind band, the military band, and in numerous types of ensembles. They also feature as solo instruments. Orchestral brass normally include B flat trumpets, French horns, tenor trombones, bass trombone and tuba, although other brass instruments, such as the B flat cornet, have occasionally been used in the orchestra. Accomplished performers on some brass instruments may be able to exceed the instrumental ranges shown here. Students, however, are advised to keep well within the limit specified when writing for brass instruments.

E flat soprano cornet

The E flat soprano cornet is mainly found in the military band, the concert wind band and the brass band. It is smaller and higher pitched than the B flat cornet, and is a transposing instrument. It sounds a minor 3rd higher than written.

B flat cornet

The B flat cornet features mostly in music for bands. It is a transposing instrument, sounding a major 2nd lower than written. Its range is similar to the B flat trumpet, although the tone of the cornet is more mellow.

B flat trumpet

The B flat trumpet is widely used in the orchestra and in bands. It is a transposing instrument, sounding a major 2nd lower than written.

B flat flugelhorn

The B flat flugelhorn, or **flugelhorn**, is sometimes referred to as the **alto flugel horn** or **flugel**. It is similar in design to the B flat cornet, although it has a wider bore (or tubing),

and its tone is somewhat more mellow. The B flat flugelhorn is found particularly in the brass band. It is a transposing instrument, sounding a major 2nd lower than written.

Horn in F or French horn

The **Horn in F**, or **French horn**, is an orchestral instrument also found in the military and concert wind band, but not in the brass band. It is a transposing instrument sounding a perfect 5th lower than written. While music for French horn can use the treble and bass clef, it is customary to use only the treble clef in music for band.

E flat horn or tenor horn

The E flat horn or tenor horn, sometimes also referred to as the **alto saxhorn**, is found particularly in the brass band. The tenor horn is similar in shape, although smaller than, the euphonium, baritone and tuba. It is a transposing instrument, written in the treble clef and sounding a major 6th lower.

B flat baritone

The B flat baritone or **B flat baritone saxhorn** features particularly in the military band, the concert wind band and the brass band. Music for the B flat baritone may be written in the following ways:

- As a transposing instrument in B flat, the treble clef is used, and the instrument sounds a major 9th lower than written.
- As a non-transposing instrument, the bass clef is used and the instrument sounds at the written pitch.

B flat euphonium

While the B flat euphonium, sometimes referred to as a **tenor tuba**, occasionally appears in the orchestra, it is mainly found in the military band, the concert wind band and the brass band. The euphonium is similar in shape, range and pitch to the B flat baritone, although its larger bore (or tubing) gives the B flat euphonium a broader and more mellow sound.

As with the B flat baritone, music for the B flat euphonium may be written either in the treble clef, sounding a major 9th below, or in the bass clef, sounding at the written pitch.

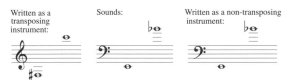

B flat tenor trombone

The B flat tenor trombone is found in the orchestra, as well as in a wide variety of bands and ensembles. Music for the B flat tenor trombone is written both in the bass and tenor clef, sounding as written, as if it were a non-transposing instrument. However, in brass band music, the B flat tenor trombone is treated as a transposing instrument, and its part is written in the treble clef, but sounding a major 9th lower than written.

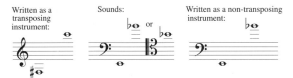

Three deep pedal notes below the ordinary compass are obtainable:

The tenor-bass trombone or B flat / F trombone

The tenor-bass trombone or B flat / F trombone is a B flat tenor trombone, with an "F attachment" (an extra coil of tubing, connected through a rotary valve operated by the left thumb) which extends the available lower notes down to C. The B flat / F trombone, therefore, covers the range of both tenor and bass trombone and is now widely used in the orchestra and band. It is treated as a non-transposing instrument.

Written and sounds:

The **B flat / F / E trombone** with an additional thumb valve and wider bore is principally used as a bass trombone.

Bass trombone in G

The bass trombone in G is pitched a minor 3rd below the B flat tenor trombone, and is treated as a non-transposing instrument. Music for the bass trombone in G is written in the bass clef. The bass trombone in G is now rarely used.

Written and sounds:

Tuba

There are several different types of tuba, which all generally fulfil the same role in the orchestra or band. The orchestral tuba is usually the **tuba in F, tuba in C, tuba in E flat** or **tuba in B flat**. All are written in the bass clef and are treated as non-transposing instruments. In the brass band, military band and concert wind band, tubas are usually referred to as **basses**. These bands use the **E flat bass** and the **B flat bass** (or **BB flat bass** meaning **double B flat bass**). The name **bombardon** has also been applied to the tubas as used in the band.

Tubas made in circular form, as distinct from the upright form, are called **helicons**, the most popular being the **sousaphone** which originated in America. This instrument, circling the player's body and carried over the shoulder, has a large forward-facing bell. The sousaphone is found in dance bands and marching bands.

When writing music for the E flat bass or the B flat bass in the military or concert wind band, the bass clef is used and the instruments are treated as non-transposing. When writing for the basses in the brass band, they are treated as transposing instruments and written in the treble clef. In this case, the E flat bass sounds a major 13th lower than written, and the B flat bass sounds two octaves plus a major 2nd lower than written.

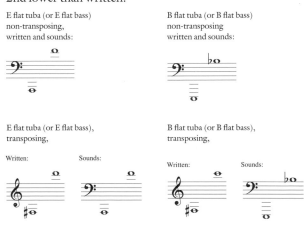

27
Percussion instruments

Percussion instruments are those instruments which are sounded by striking or shaking. Although there is a great variety of percussion instruments, they may be categorised as those which produce notes of definite pitch, and those which produce notes of indefinite pitch.

Instruments which produce notes of definite pitch include **timpani** (**kettle-drums**), **glockenspiel, bell lyra, vibraphone, xylophone, marimba, celesta** and **tubular bells**.

Instruments which produce notes of indefinite pitch include **bass drum, tenor drum, side drum, tom-tom, bongo drum, cymbal, gong, triangle, tambourine, castanets, maracas** and **claves**.

Instruments of definite pitch

Timpani

Timpani, or **kettle-drums**, are considered the most important percussion instruments in the orchestra. These large drums are seldom used singly. At least two kettle-drums are usually used together: a smaller one for the higher notes and a larger one for the lower notes. Often three or four kettle-drums are used, and occasionally even more are required.

The larger kettle-drum has this range:

The smaller kettle-drum has this range:

The range of a pair of kettle-drums may be slightly extended by the addition of larger or smaller drums.

Music for timpani is traditionally written without key signatures and without accidentals, with the required pitch or tuning written at the beginning of the music, like this:

The drum roll is particularly effective on timpani, and is written like this:

or this:

The first of these two notations of the drum roll is preferred.

Dynamic marks, carefully added to the timpani part, further increase the effectiveness of the instrument. For example, the drum roll performed with a **crescendo** or a **diminuendo** can have dramatic effect:

The tuning of modern timpani is controlled by a pedal, which also makes the **glissando** possible (a smooth sliding effect from note to note).

Glockenspiel

The glockenspiel has a set of tuned steel bars of varying length, which are struck with (usually one or two) sticks or beaters to produce a bell-like sound. Glockenspiels appear in a variety of ranges, although two sizes, each with a chromatic range, are most common. The range of the smaller of these two instruments is given below. Music for glockenspiel is written in the treble clef two octaves below the actual pitch. The **bell lyra**, or **lyre bells**, found in the marching band is a portable form of glockenspiel.

The **vibraphone** has a set of tuned metal bars of varying length, but underneath each metal bar is a resonator tube. The range of the vibraphone is from F below middle C, upwards for three octaves, sounding at its written pitch.

Xylophone

The xylophone has a set of tuned wooden bars of varying length, and is played with sticks or beaters in the same way as the glockenspiel. Xylophones vary in size and range, although a compass of between two and three octaves is usual. Music for xylophone is usually written in the treble clef one octave below the actual pitch, although occasionally it can be written at its actual pitch.

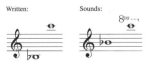

The **marimba** has a set of tuned wooden bars of varying length, and underneath each wooden bar is a resonator tube. The range of the marimba varies, although a compass from the C below middle C upwards for three octaves is not uncommon. It is written at its actual pitch. The compass of the **bass marimba** often extends upwards from the C two octaves below middle C.

Celesta

The celesta is a small keyboard instrument. It consists of a set of metal bars, which are struck by hammers operated by a keyboard. The instrument, which may be described as a keyboard glockenspiel, produces clear, delicate bell-like sounds. A well-known example of its use is in the *Dance of the Sugar-Plum Fairy* in Tchaikovsky's *Nutcracker Suite*. Music for the celesta is written on two bracketed staves as for the piano, but one octave below its actual pitch.

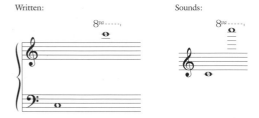

Tubular bells

Tubular bells or **chimes** are a set of tuned metal tubes of varying length which are suspended from a frame and hit with a wooden mallet. The range of the tubular bells varies. The normal compass of 18 chromatic notes is illustrated here. Music for tubular bells is written in the treble clef.

Instruments of indefinite pitch

Notation

There are different ways in which music for percussion instruments of indefinite pitch can be notated. The music may be written on the stave, with a treble or bass clef. For example:

Sometimes the clef is omitted. When the stave is used, several instruments may also share the one stave, with each instrument written in a different space (or on a different line). For example:

Often, instead of writing music for percussion instruments of indefinite pitch on the stave, a single line is used for one or two instruments, like this:

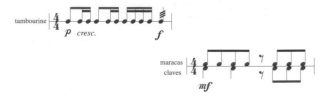

A drum roll is indicated in the same manner as for timpani, written in one of the following ways:

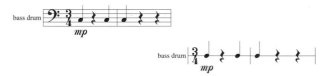

Bass drum

The bass drum is a large drum, varying considerably in size. In orchestral and some band music, the bass drum is hit with one or two sticks or beaters. When the bass drum is played as part of a drum kit, it is struck by a beater connected to a mechanical foot pedal. Music for bass drum is either notated in the bass clef, in the third space down, with the note stem upwards, or on a single line:

When the bass drum shares the stave with the side (or snare) drum, and/or cymbals, the bass drum part is written in the third space down or in the lowest space on the stave, with its note stems downwards, with or without a bass clef.

Tenor drum

The tenor drum is midway in size between the side drum and the bass drum. Unlike the side drum, it does not have snares. The tenor drum is rarely used in the orchestra. Its part can be written on the stave, or on a single line.

Side drum

The side drum or **snare** drum is a small drum. Gut or wire snares produce the characteristic rattling sound when the drum is struck. The snares are strung across the lower of the two drum heads. They can be lifted clear or removed from the drum head if required. Music for side drum is usually notated either on the stave in the second space down with note stems downwards and with a treble clef, or on a single line. When sharing a stave with the bass drum or cymbal, music for the side drum is written in the second space down on the stave, with or without a bass clef.

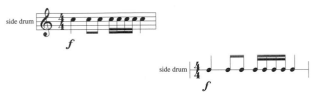

Tom-tom

Usually found in sets of two or more, the tom-tom drum appears in a variety of sizes, and often as part of the modern drum kit. Music for tom-tom can be notated in several ways:

- Written on the stave, with or without a bass clef, in the second space down. (1)
- Written on a single line. (2)
- Drum kit notation often places the small tom-tom part in the top space of the stave with its stems upwards, and the floor tom-tom (or large tom-tom) in the third space down with its note stems upwards. (3)
- Music for two tom-toms can be written using the top two spaces of the stave (or above and below a single line). (4)

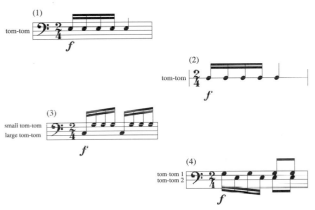

Bongo drum

Usually found in sets of two, bongos are small drums struck with the fingers or with sticks.

Cymbal

The cymbal, a circular brass plate, comes in many sizes and is played in several ways. A single cymbal may be suspended and struck with one or two sticks, while two cymbals of equal size may be hand-held and clashed together. **Hi-hat** cymbals are two cymbals of equal size mounted on a stand and operated by a foot pedal, usually as part of the drum kit. Music for cymbal can be notated in several ways:

- Written on a single line:

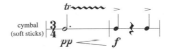

- Written on a single line but with diamond shaped note-heads or crosses:

- Written in the top space of the stave with a bass clef. In orchestral music, the cymbal sometimes shares the stave with the bass drum:

- In music for drum kit, the cymbal part is written in the top space of the stave and/or in the space just above the stave, usually notated by crosses:

- The hi-hat cymbal played with the foot can be notated as follows:

Drum kit

The drum kit includes **bass drum**, **snare drum** and **cymbals**, with a variety of other drums and cymbals often added. It is customary to write music for the drum kit on one stave, with or without a bass clef. However, there are many different ways of writing a score for drum kit as the following notation illustrates:

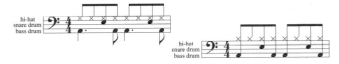

1: bass drum 2: snare drum 3 & 4: small tom-tom 5 & 6: larger tom-tom 7 & 8: large or floor tom-tom 9: crash cymbal or hi-hat cymbal 10: crash cymbal 11: ride cymbal 12: ride cymbal or hi-hat cymbal 13: open hi-hat cymbal 14: closed hi-hat cymbal 15 & 16: hi-hat cymbal played with foot.

Whichever notation you use, always indicate on the music which instruments are required. This will avoid any confusion. The following examples show two slightly different ways of writing for bass drum, snare drum and hi-hat cymbal.

When a number of percussion instruments of indefinite pitch share one stave, it may not be possible, or necessary, to include every rest for each instrument. Sticks, brushes or specific types of beater should be specified where appropriate.

Gong

The gong or **tam-tam** is a large heavy metal disc, with its edge turned over. It is suspended in a frame and hit with a soft-headed drumstick or beater. The part for gong is usually written on one line without a clef:

Triangle

The triangle is a small steel rod bent in the shape of a triangle, open at one angle. It is struck with a metal beater. The part for triangle is written either on the stave with a treble clef, in the second space down, or on a single line like this:

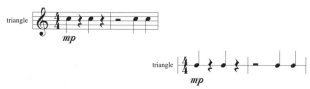

Diamond shaped note-heads or crosses may also be used to notate the triangle part:

The **tremolo** or **roll**, made by rapidly striking two sides of the instrument alternately, is notated like this:

Tambourine

The tambourine is a small single-headed drum, with jingles (small metal plates) inserted around the edge. The tambourine part may be written like this:

Castanets

Castanets are two small hollow pieces of hard wood, clicked together by the fingers or fastened to the end of a stick which is shaken. A single line can be used for the castanets part:

Maracas

The maraca is a gourd filled with dried seeds which rattle when the instrument is shaken. Often used in pairs, the maracas part is written like this:

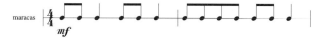

Claves

Claves are a pair of hard-wood sticks which are beaten together. Their part can be written like this:

28
Keyboard instruments

There is a great variety of keyboard instruments including those with:

- strings which are plucked (**harpsichord**, **spinet**, **virginals**) or struck (**clavichord** and **piano**)
- pipes or reeds through which air passes (**pipe organ, harmonium, piano-accordion**)
- metal bars struck by hammers (**celesta**)
- sounds which are produced electronically (**electronic keyboard, electronic organ, digital piano, synthesizer**)

The piano, pipe organ, electronic keyboard, synthesizer and digital piano are described here. The celesta is described on page 200.

The piano

The full name for the piano is the **pianoforte**. It has a series of strings which are stretched over a sound-board, and struck by felt-headed hammers. The hammers are connected to the keyboard through a complex mechanism called the **action**. High notes have three strings tuned to the same pitch, notes in the middle range have two strings, and low notes have one string. The metal frame to which the strings are attached is fixed either horizontally, as in the **grand piano**, or vertically, as in the **upright piano**. The compass of the modern piano is usually seven or seven-and-a-quarter octaves, much greater than the range of the earlier instruments. Music for piano is usually written on two bracketed staves. Sometimes three staves are used, but this is rare.

Written and sounds:

The piano has two, or sometimes three, pedals. The left pedal, often referred to as the **soft pedal**, is operated by the left foot and lessens the volume. On the grand piano, the left pedal moves the hammers and the keyboard slightly sideways, so that the hammers strike only two strings (instead of three), or one string (instead of two) for each note. On the upright piano, the left pedal brings the hammers nearer to the strings. The instruction to depress the left pedal is **una corda**, and to release it, **tre corda**. The right pedal, called the **damper pedal** or **sustaining pedal**, is operated by the right foot. When depressed, this pedal holds the dampers away from the strings leaving all the strings free to vibrate, and prolonging the sound. To indicate when the damper pedal should be depressed and released, either of the following directions can be written beneath the lower stave of the piano music:

℘ed.   ✳ or P _____

Occasionally, when the damper pedal is required, indicated by directions **con ped.**, or **col ped.**, exact pedal markings are omitted. The use of the pedal is then left to the performer's discretion. On some pianos there is a third pedal, called the **sostenuto pedal**, found between the other two pedals. When this pedal is depressed, only the notes already sounding are sustained, while subsequent notes can be played without being sustained.

The organ

The pipe organ is a keyboard instrument consisting of rows, or **ranks**, of pipes of different sizes, which sound as air passes through them. Each rank provides a complete range of notes of a particular tone quality. Most pipe organs have more than one keyboard, or **manual**. While two-manual organs are most frequently used, instruments with up to five manuals are not uncommon. The organ also has a **pedal-board**, which is played by the feet. The pedal-board and each manual control ranks of pipes.

The manuals are named. On a two-manual organ, the lower manual is called the **Great Organ** and the upper manual is the **Swell Organ**. Where there is a third manual, below the Great, it is called the **Choir Organ**. A fourth manual, above the Swell, is called the **Solo Organ**.

Each rank of pipes is called a **stop**, and these are of various pitches and lengths. An **eight-foot (8′) stop** produces sounds at the 'normal' pitch, corresponding, for example, to the notes on a piano. A **four-foot (4′) stop** uses pipes sounding one octave above the 8′ pitch, and a **two-foot (2′) stop** sounds two octaves above the 8′ pitch. A **16-foot (16′) stop** uses pipes sounding one octave lower than the 8′ pitch, and a **32-foot (32′) stop** sounds two octaves lower than the 8′ pitch.

Mutation stops sound at intervals other than the octave, such as a 12th, and, when combined with 8′ stops, add brilliance. **Mixture stops** have two or more pipes, including mutation pipes, to each note.

While the written range of the organ is less than the piano, the actual range is far greater, due to the combination of pipe lengths that may be used. Three staves are used for organ music; the upper two for the manuals and the lower one for the pedal-board.

Electronic keyboard

There are many different types of electronic keyboard. The variety is so great that it is impractical to give other than general information here. These keyboards all produce their sounds electronically, and even the smaller instruments produce a wide range of pitch, timbre, effects and rhythms. The compass of the keyboard varies greatly, although instruments with four or five octaves are the standard sizes. Some electronic keyboard instruments, such as the digital piano, may have a keyboard compass of up to just over seven octaves. The actual range of sounds, however, may extend far beyond the actual compass of the keyboard.

Many electronic keyboards are so versatile that it is difficult, and unnecessary, to categorise them. However, there are some distinctions in this group of instruments. While the name **electronic keyboard** refers to a variety of instruments, it also refers more specifically to those instruments often called **portable keyboards**. They have pre-set voices and rhythms, and can produce single-finger chords. Many electronic keyboards have additional functions including pre-programmed accompaniments and chord sequences, with memory and multi-track facilities. Some also have drum pads and touch-sensitive keyboards and are multi-timbral and computer-compatible.

Synthesizers produce an extremely wide range of sounds, often with editing facilities, and are computer-compatible. In general, they do not feature pre-set rhythms and single-finger functions, but many are multi-timbral and have touch-sensitive keyboards.

Digital pianos provide authentic piano sounds with weighted keyboards. They often have additional voices and are computer-compatible.

The **electronic organ**, complete with manuals and pedal-board, often now replaces the church pipe organ, and produces a powerful and authentic sound. A smaller version of the electronic organ, often with two manuals and a pedal-board, is popular for home use.

Music for electronic keyboard is written on two bracketed staves, like piano music, sometimes with added chord symbols. (1) It can also be written on a single stave with treble clef and chord symbols (2).

Music for electronic organ is normally written on three staves, the upper two for the manuals and the lower stave for the pedal-board.

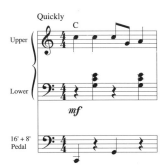

Sometimes, music for electronic organ is written on two staves. The upper stave is used for the upper manual, while the lower stave is used for the lower manual and the pedal-board. Information about voicings may also be included, whether the music is written on two or three staves:

Upper : string ensemble and piano
Lower : flutes and strings
Pedal : 16' and 8'
Drums : samba   ♩ = 120

29
How to set out your music

When writing for instruments and voices, it is important to know how to set out the music. For many ensembles, such as a vocal duet, piano trio, string quartet or orchestra, the full score of the music is usually set out with instruments or voices written in a particular order. While there may be some flexibility and variation in the ways in which music is set out for larger ensembles, such as the brass band or concert wind band, students are advised to follow the guidelines suggested here.

However, while the following information provides a quick reference as to how to set out your music, it is not practicable to show every possible combination of voices and instruments here, nor give other than general guidance on good practice. You should take every opportunity to study printed scores, and always consult them if in doubt about points of procedure and presentation.

The first page

The first page of a score should contain the **title of the music** and the **name of the composer**. It should also be made clear for which instrument(s) or voice(s) the music is written. When the music has more than one instrumental or vocal part, the name of each instrument or voice should be written before the stave on which its music appears. You should also indicate the **tempo** (speed) of the music. This is written above the top stave at the beginning of the music. The appropriate **clef(s)**, **key signature**, **time signature** and **dynamic marks** should also be added to your score.

Vocal music

Unaccompanied vocal solo or unison voices

Vocal solo or unison voices with piano accompaniment

Vocal duet or two-part choir with piano accompaniment

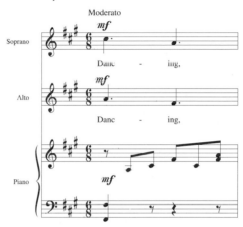

In the examples for vocal solo and duet, the treble clef has been used for each vocal part. When a vocal part is written in the bass clef, its stave still appears above the piano staves (and not below them).

Vocal trio or three-part choir with piano accompaniment

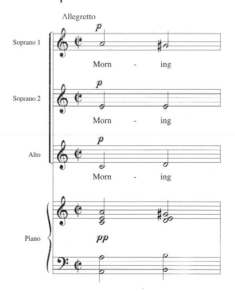

Vocal quartet or four-part choir written in short score

When the four vocal parts are written on two staves, in short score, the stems of the soprano and tenor notes always go upwards, and the alto and bass note stems always go downwards. The words may be written between the staves (example **a**) or above the top stave (example **b**), with each word or syllable written above and/or below the notes to which it must be sung.

Often, hymns written on two staves do not include the words in between or above the staves (example **c**); instead, the words of all the verses appear together, separate from the music. It is, however, helpful to write the words underneath the notes.

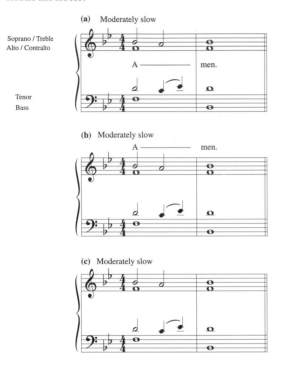

Vocal quartet or four-part choir written in open score

In open score, each part is written on a separate stave. Barlines may be written on each vocal stave separately (aligned correctly) or as continuous lines passing through all the vocal staves as shown in the examples (d) and (e).

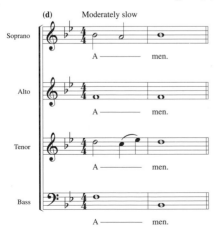

Vocal quartet or four-part choir with piano accompaniment

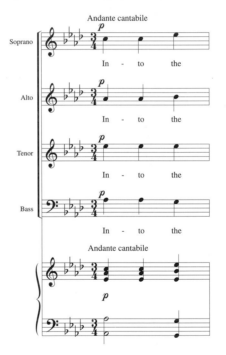

Instrumental music

Unaccompanied instrumental solo

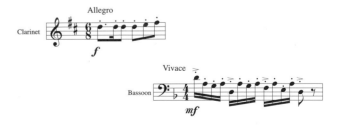

Electronic keyboard

Piano or keyboard instrument

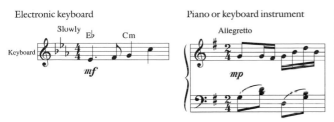

Music for more than one instrument

Duets

Instrumental solo with piano accompaniment

Duet for flute and guitar

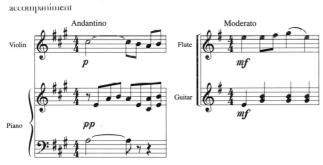

Duet for two clarinets

Duet for two cellos

Trios

String trio

Piano trio

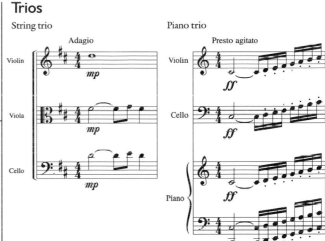

Percussion trio for snare drum, tenor drum and bass drum

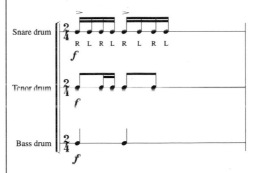

or

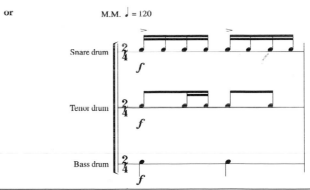

Piano duet

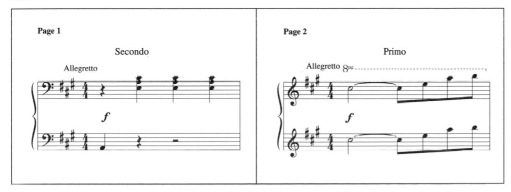

Music for piano duet is written on two facing pages. The lower part is called **secondo** and is written on the left hand page. The upper part is called **primo** and is written on the right hand page. For ease of page-turning, it is helpful to the performers if you keep exactly the same number of bars on each page.

Trio for oboe, flute and piano

Quartets

String quartet

Woodwind quartet

Brass quartet

Saxophone quartet

Quintets

String quintet. Alternatively, the string quintet may include two violins, one viola and two cellos.

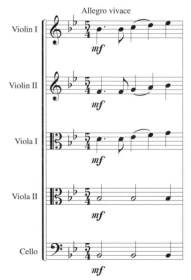

Brass quintet

Wind quintet

Piano quintet

Rock / pop group 1

Rock / pop group 2

At a moderate speed

Larger instrumental ensembles

Classroom ensemble

Instruments in classroom ensemble

Melody parts:	recorder, chime bars, xylophone, glockenspiel, electronic keyboard, or any non-transposing instrument
Chords:	guitar, electronic keyboard
Bass:	bass guitar, electronic keyboard, bass metallophone, bass xylophone
Untuned percussion 1:	triangle, tambourine, claves, castanets
Untuned percussion 2:	side drum, bongo drum
Untuned percussion 3:	tenor drum, bass drum

Piano or electronic keyboard

Rock / pop group 3

drawn through all the staves linking them together. In addition to this line, a **second line** is drawn through the staves to indicate instrumental family groups such as strings, woodwind, brass and percussion in the orchestra, or like-instruments such as cornets, horns, trombones, etc. in the brass band. This second line is discontinued between the different groups. With the exception of the continuous line which links all the staves at the beginning of each page, all other bar-lines are then only drawn through the family groups, or like-instrument groups.

If your full score manuscript paper has a sufficient number of staves, you may leave a blank stave between each group of instruments. If you have not used a full page of manuscript paper, and there is adequate space left, use it to write the next set of staves. To show that the sets of staves (or **systems**) follow on from one another and are not to be played together, two diagonal lines are drawn between each set, like this:

Band and orchestral scores

The first page of a full score should contain staves with **clef, key signature** and **time signature** for all the instruments which are required, even if they do not all play at the beginning of the music. Subsequent pages need only contain the staves for those instruments which are employed at that time, unless you are writing on manuscript paper with pre-printed names and staves.

On each page, at the very beginning of the staves (before the clefs are positioned), a **continuous line** should be

Brass band

There are usually twenty-four players in a brass band. The instruments are:
E flat soprano cornet
Solo B flat cornet
Repiano B flat cornet
2nd B flat cornet
3rd B flat cornet
B flat flugelhorn
Solo E flat tenor horn
1st E flat tenor horn
2nd E flat tenor horn
1st B flat baritone
2nd B flat baritone
B flat euphonium
1st B flat tenor trombone
2nd B flat tenor trombone
Bass trombone
E♭ flat bass
B♭ flat bass
Percussion

There are different ways to set out a full score for the brass band. One method frequently used, is shown.

A **condensed score** and **conductor's copy** of the brass band music can be written on two staves, or sometimes on three staves if percussion parts are added. When two staves with treble and bass clef are used (example **a**), the music is written at **concert pitch** (the pitch at which the music sounds). Alternatively, the music can be written on two staves, each with a treble clef (example **b**) and in the same key as the B flat instruments.

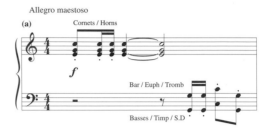

Military band, concert wind band (or symphonic wind band) and marching band

All these large ensembles, the military band, concert wind band and marching band, include woodwind and brass instruments with percussion.

The **military band**, associated with the Armed Forces, has a wide repertoire, including concert music and music performed on the march. Military bands vary in size, and several may be combined to produce very large ensembles.

The **concert wind band** or **symphonic wind** band, as the name implies, performs concert music and does not march. The instruments and numbers in these ensembles vary considerably.

The **marching band** is particularly notable in the USA, and has a smaller range of instruments than the symphonic wind band, the main consideration being the suitability of the instruments to be played outdoors on the march.

The following instruments may be found in the above named ensembles:

- C piccolo, D flat piccolo, flute, G alto flute,
- oboe, cor anglais,
- E flat clarinet, B flat clarinets (solo, 1st, 2nd, 3rd), E flat alto clarinet, B flat bass clarinet, B flat contrabass clarinet,
- bassoon, double bassoon,

- E flat alto saxophone (1st, 2nd), B flat tenor saxophone,
  E flat baritone saxophone, B flat bass saxophone,
- E flat cornet, B flat cornets (1st, 2nd, 3rd),
- B flat trumpet, B flat flugelhorn
- horns in F (1st, 2nd, 3rd, 4th), horns in E flat (1st, 2nd,
  3rd, 4th),
- B flat baritone, B flat euphonium,
- B flat trombone (1st, 2nd), bass trombone,
- B flat basses / tubas, E flat basses / tubas

A wide variety of percussion instruments may be added,
including timpani, bass drum, side drum, cymbals, tubular
bells, glockenspiel, xylophone, marimba, claves, tambourine, maracas, triangle, wood block and gong. The double bass and the electric bass guitar are also used in the band.

There are several ways to set out music for these bands.
The instruments in the score will depend upon the type and
size of band for which you are writing. The following score
shows a typical combination of instruments in a concert
wind band:

A condensed score or conductor's copy of the music for military band,
concert wind band and marching band may be written on two, three or
four staves, as appropriate.

The orchestra

The orchestra has developed over a period of more than two hundred years. The modern orchestra, with its four sections of strings, woodwind, brass and percussion, appeared by the end of the eighteenth century. However, the early orchestra was much smaller than today's, and did not contain the number and variety of instruments that are presently used.

The string orchestra

The string orchestra consists of violins (divided into first and second violins), violas, cellos and double basses. In some music, the double basses share a stave with the cellos, when both play the same part, although the double bass sounds one octave lower. Music written before the nineteenth century was often scored in this way. If the double bass part is independent from the cello part, add a separate stave for it.

The early modern orchestra or classical orchestra

The orchestras for which Franz Joseph Haydn (1732–1809) and Wolfgang Amadeus Mozart (1756–1791) wrote were much smaller than today's orchestras. During this period, the combination of instruments found in the orchestra became standardised. By 1800, the orchestra usually contained the following instruments:

Strings: violins (1st and 2nd), violas, cellos, double basses
Woodwind: 2 flutes, 2 oboes, 2 clarinets, 2 bassoons
Brass: 2 horns, 2 trumpets
Percussion: 2 kettle drums (timpani)

Symphony no. 104 in D ('London') (1st movement)
J Haydn

Larger orchestras

Throughout the nineteenth century and into the early twentieth century, the orchestra grew in size. New instruments were added to the list of instruments found in the classical orchestra, as composers called for larger and more powerful orchestras. Study a number of scores of orchestral music written during the last 200 years to see how the orchestra has developed. To illustrate this, here are some lists of the instruments required to perform six pieces of orchestral music:

Franz Josef Haydn
1732 - 1809

Symphony No. 104 in D

Composed 1795

2 Flutes
2 Oboes
2 Clarinets
2 Bassoons

2 Horns
2 Trumpets

2 Timpani

Violins I
Violins II
Violas
Cellos
Double basses

Ludwig van Beethoven
1770 - 1827

Overture: Leonore No. 3

Composed 1806

2 Flutes
2 Oboes
2 Clarinets
2 Bassoons

4 Horns
2 Trumpets
3 Trombones

2 Timpani

Violins I
Violins II
Violas
Cellos
Double basses

Richard Wagner
1813 - 1883

*Overture: The Mastersingers of
    Nuremburg*

Composed between 1861 and 1867;
    first performed 1868

Piccolo
2 Flutes
2 Oboes
2 Clarinets
2 Bassoons

4 Horns
3 Trumpets
3 Trombones

2 Timpani
Triangle
Cymbals

Harp

Violins I
Violins II
Violas
Cellos
Double basses

Antonin Dvořák
1841 - 1904

*Symphony No. 9 in E minor
    (From the New World)*

Composed 1893

Piccolo
2 Flutes
2 Oboes

Cor anglais

2 Clarinets

2 Bassoons

4 Horns
2 Trumpets
3 Trombones
Tuba

2 Timpani

Triangle
Cymbals

Violins I
Violins II
Violas
Cellos
Double basses

Edward Elgar
1857 - 1934

Symphony No. 2 in E flat

Composed 1910

Piccolo
3 Flutes
2 Oboes

Cor anglais

3 Clarinets
Bass Clarinet
2 Bassoons
Double bassoon

4 Horns
3 Trumpets
3 Trombones
Tuba

3 Timpani
Bass drum
Side drum

Cymbals
Tambourine

2 Harps

Violins I
Violins II
Violas
Cellos
Double basses

Maurice Ravel
1875 - 1937

Bolero

Composed 1928

Piccolo
2 Flutes
2 Oboes
Oboe d'amore
Cor anglais
E♭ Clarinet
2 Clarinets (B♭)
Bass Clarinet
2 Bassoons
Double bassoon

4 Horns
4 Trumpets
3 Trombones
Tuba
3 Saxophones

3 Timpani
Bass drum
2 Side drum

Cymbals

Tam-tam
Celesta

Harp

Violins I
Violins II
Violas
Cellos
Double basses

Orchestra with solo instruments

If there is a solo instrument playing with the orchestra, such as the violin in a violin concerto, the solo part is always written on the score below the percussion instruments, but above the strings. The full score should be organised in this order:

Woodwind
Brass
Percussion
Solo instrument
Strings

Orchestra with voices

Vocal parts for solo voice(s) and/or choir are also written on the full score below the percussion instruments and above the strings:

Woodwind
Brass
Percussion
Solo voice(s)
Choir
Strings

Index